A SECOND TOUCH

A SECOND TOUCH

By KEITH MILLER

WORD BOOKS
LONDON

Grateful acknowledgment is made to the following for permission to use copyright material:

CAMBRIDGE UNIVERSITY PRESS
A quotation from *The New English Bible, New Testament,* ©
The Delegates of the Oxford University Press and the Syndics of the Cambridge University Press 1961. Used by permission.

THE DIVISION OF CHRISTIAN EDUCATION OF THE NATIONAL COUNCIL OF CHURCHES OF CHRIST
Quotations from The Revised Standard Version of the Bible, Copyright © 1946 and 1952.

HARPER AND ROW, PUBLISHERS, INCORPORATED
The quotation from *Theory of Psychoanalytic Techniques* by Karl Menninger. Copyright © 1964.

HARPER AND ROW, PUBLISHERS, INCORPORATED
Quotations from *Guilt and Grace* by Paul Tournier, Copyright © 1962.

THE MACMILLAN COMPANY
Quotations from *The Ring of Truth* by J. B. Phillips, Copyright © 1967 by J. B. Phillips. Used by permission.

BEACON PRESS
A quotation from *Man's Search For Meaning* by Viktor E. Frankl, Copyright © 1964.

Paperback Edition—1st printing April 1971
2nd printing August 1971
3rd printing December 1972
published by WORD BOOKS, London,
a Division of Word (U.K.) Ltd, Park Lane,
Hemel Hempstead, Hertfordshire

ISBN 0 85009 027 X

Printed in Malta by St Paul's Press Ltd

INTRODUCTION

This is a sequel to *The Taste of New Wine*. The areas of life dealt with are different; the over-all purpose is to approach certain problems of renewal in the institutional Church from a personal perspective. But in order to try to approach institutional life from this direction, I find that I must first try to describe, portray, and illustrate in detail the *particular perspective* from which I am beginning to see the 'Christian life'.

This is not a book for atheists. It is for those of you who have tried to live your faith in God in the context of the Christian Church—but who have become frustrated, lonely, or anxious in your trying.

In my mind, as I write this, I am inviting you to come into my inner life. As you look through my eyes with me at these pages, I hope you will discover what I am beginning to discover about living for Christ in the world and in the Church. In a very real way I *need* some of you to see what I am seeing. I have felt alone in so many of my struggles to find meaning and to be God's person that I find I am writing this to those of you who also sometimes feel alone and discouraged as Christians.

The book is in three parts. The first was written to describe the dawning consciousness that for me the

Christian life was beginning to look different, several
years after a 'new commitment'. I was finding a new perspective. The second part consists of looking through
this perspective at commonly held assumptions and describing my 'new' perceptions in the context of ordinary
living. And in the final section I have asked you to come
with me back into the institutional Church and look with
new eyes at the problems and hope for Renewal. The
second part is the longest since I feel that so many renewal efforts have failed, not essentially because of bad
programmes, but because of the lack of a *common motivating vision of the Christian life* in the thinking of the
'renewers'.

A Second Touch is not a substitute way which bypasses the beginning commitment of the Christian life or
the necessary acquiring of habits of personal prayer,
study of the Scriptures, and worship . . . as well as broad-
ening studies of all kinds about the world. I have assumed you know that I believe it to be a *continuing
necessity* to immerse one's self in these fundamental disciplines. As a matter of fact, my past attempts to bypass
or dispense with these disciplines have invariably led to
miserable periods of emotional subjectivism. But I feel
that, sooner or later, the practice of Christian disciplines
should contribute to an overall style of thinking through
which God expands one's total consciousness and pushes
back the horizons of one's 'Christian life'. And through
this new awareness I believe Christians may see *all of life*
—including the Church—from a new perspective.

The title came from reading the story of Jesus' healing
of the blind man—the way He touched his eyes and
asked him,

'Can you see at all?' The man looked up and said,

'I can see people. But they look like trees walking around.' So Jesus touched his eyes a second time—and then he saw men as Christ saw them.[1]

1. See Mark 8:23–25.

ACKNOWLEDGMENTS

So many people have helped me personally through the past two years that I feel as if this book should have a group signature. I am an intuitive blotter. All my life I have absorbed ideas unconsciously which have later come to the surface of my consciousness as my own. How general this is I don't know. All I can say is that where I have consciously and specifically borrowed an idea, I have given credit. Many of the thoughts set out here came from the men who meet at 6.30 on Monday mornings at Walter Carrington's office to pray. I am particularly grateful to Charles Sumners and Brooks Goldsmith from that group, who took the time to read this book in manuscript form and who offered valuable suggestions. But it has been the experience of living with all those men which has made me really believe that life in the Church can be made new.

Gene Warr, Elton Trueblood, Bruce Larson, Wally Howard, Charles Huffman, and Virginia Sumners were very helpful in different ways. Each took time out of an extremely busy schedule to read or discuss all or parts of this manuscript and to render aid. However, none of them is responsible for the mistakes in style or content which the finished book may include. I feel it only fair to underline this, since there were some suggestions offered which, if followed, would have made this a totally different book.

I am grateful to Barbara Lord and Vivian Whitehead for typing various drafts and to Vi White for her help in the library. Also I want to thank Emma Ward for being secretary, sounding board and friend in the preparation of the final draft—and my friend, Blake Gillen, for his encouragement and for providing a quiet place to write.

And finally, I am most grateful to my wife, Mary Allen, and our three girls, for all kinds of support and help with the writing and correction of the book, and for their willingness for me to share some of our personal life together with you, in the hope that all of us can be brought closer to God and each other through our common pilgrimage.

KEITH MILLER

To

Leslie, Kristin, and Mary-Keith

CONTENTS

Part I

BEGINNING TO SEE FROM A NEW

VANTAGE POINT

Chapter I

A NEW PERSPECTIVE

'... be transformed by the renewal of your mind ...'
Romans 12: 2 (RSV)

I do not even recall how it started, but it was bad. We were really mad at each other. I remember estimating to myself that it was probably going to be at least one of those 'three day mads'. But there was a hard quality about this time that I did not like at all. We had already been through the open hostility stage. Direct verbal communication had stopped, except for those crisp, necessary exchanges which allow the flow of life with its car sharing, etc., to go on. When guests came on Saturday, I remember being amazed to see us responding to them in a perfectly natural way . . . and even to each other in the presence of the guests. After they left, silence dropped again. All Saturday evening and Sunday after church we worked around the garden and house. At meals we spoke through the children and shot each other down with glances over their heads.

By Sunday night we were both exhausted. I wanted to be alone, but to leave Mary Allen with the children would *prove* I was unreasonable and selfish. Finally, I had a plan. I would suggest that the two of us go to the cinema. She does not like to go to see a film when she is very tired, so she would refuse, and I could go on alone. But Mary Allen is very perceptive. She said she would

like to go to the cinema. The one I suggested was full, so
we went to another. This second picture was all about a
couple, both of whom did nothing but pick at each other,
resent what the other said, and express selfishness. It
was a terrible experience; the husband, who was obviously neurotic, even said some of my lines. The show
was so revealing that we didn't dare even look at each
other. After the film, we drove home . . . in silence. I
realized exactly what had happened to us. I had coun-
selled dozens of couples and had told them what I had
found to be a Christian solution for this situation for me.
I knew that one of us had to confess his own fault in the
problem, really mean it, and let the chips fall where they
might. You have to sincerely mean it because your partner may well *agree* with your confession and say that she
is 'glad you finally saw it'. But I know of no other way
than for one party to somehow see and confess something of his responsibility for the problem—even if it is
only the resentment resulting from a still unresolved
issue.

As we drove along, I considered turning on the radio,
but then decided I didn't want to argue—silently—
about the music. I saw how stubborn and self-centred I
had been, but I kept reminding myself of *her* part in all
this. 'O.K.,' I finally told myself, 'you're supposed to be
the big Christian counsellor. Let's hear you do what
you're supposed to.' But when I looked over and cleared
my throat, *I could not do it*. "I'll confess later,' I thought
to myself. But, for the first time in years, I could not. I
went to bed filled with resentment. As I lay there in the
dark, blinking back tears of rage and frustration, I
realized again that I was a helpless little boy who not only

could not do what he knew was right, but didn't want to. There was no solution.

The next morning, Monday at 6.30, a dozen of us men met, as we do every Monday morning, to pray together and discuss the experiment of faith in God to which each of us is trying to give his life. This group is made up of anything but a bunch of pious, Sunday School-types. It is almost impossible to be phoney with them. Furthermore, not only was there no 'victory' for me to report, but there was considerable doubt in my mind regarding any solution to our situation at home. I realized that I really needed their prayers, and that I was just protecting myself and my reputation as a Christian by my silence, since many of them had been honest about the pressing issues in their lives. So I told the group what I have just told you. After a couple of minutes of silence, the man sitting next to me quietly confessed that he had had a remarkably similar weekend. Two other men then related almost identical experiences. We began to talk about our pride and our inability to overcome it. We began to see the girls' side. After we had talked awhile, my whole situation was in some way different. That morning we ended our meeting by praying for each other and anyone else in the world who might be trapped by pride.

When the meeting was over, I couldn't wait to get to the telephone. Now that I *really saw* myself, I was free to call home and tell Mary Allen how I had not been able to get through to her the night before and how sorry I was to put her through all that hell. Although there was some 'wind damage' to be cleared up, we both knew that the storm was over. As I hung up, I realized in amazement that *nothing had changed* in our situation since the night before. *Nothing* had been solved. And yet suddenly we

were both free to love each other. Not only was I free
from the particular situation, but that Monday was the
most creative day I had had in months. All kinds of fresh
insights about the work I was doing came to me without
any straining on my part. In some very important way, as
a result of the experience I had just been through, my
little world had been unlocked and was available to me
to work with. Then I began to understand.

Sunday night I had seen my world, but the people in it
were objects who would not bend to my will.

Monday morning, through those men and through our
vulnerable sharing of our real humanity with each other
and with God, Christ had touched my eyes, and for a
day, for a week, I saw the people in my world as I think
Christ sees them. Nothing was different—and yet *everything* had changed. I had been looking for days for a
plan, a little personal Christian programme to undertake,
through which my problem would be solved. But God
did not give me a plan. He gave me something infinitely
more freeing and creative. He gave me a whole new perspective.

As I thought about this experience and many more like
it in my life, I began to suspect that I had been searching
in the wrong places for personal renewal in my 'Christian life'. For years I had been trying every new technique or programme I could find that seemed to have
value, only to discover that before long each one became
a compulsive duty. And finally, many of these 'duties'
would bore me. I was afraid to admit even to myself that
prayer, for instance, sometimes bored me, so I kept
searching for new techniques and trying them.

One Sunday evening a few months ago I was sitting

with my family when the telephone rang. It was a long
distance call from another state. A young ordained
minister whom I had never met was on the line. He had
read *The Taste of New Wine*. His wife, who said she had
reviewed the book three times, was on an extension.
There was a very tired, almost wistful quality in the
young man's voice. 'What is the meaning of this crazy
Christian life, Keith? What's it really all about?' At first
I thought that it must be a joke. But in the same instant
I realized that it wasn't at all; and as he talked on, I
knew what he meant.

'Keith,' he could have said, 'what happens when a person makes a conscious attempt to commit his entire life
to the living God, lives a few joyous, productive years in
his Church—maybe even becomes an ordained minister
—and then wakes up one day and finds that the well has
gone dry. "Faith" becomes only a word again. What
kind of a Way is there for people like us—people who
have been baptized and confirmed, have practised the
Christian disciplines, and have said all the right formulas
after accepting Christ as Saviour and Lord? And yet, if
we dare to be honest, we are fed up with our *churchy*
talking, with the continual religious noise, and with the
nervous, seemingly "manufactured" involvement of our
Christian brothers. But still, beneath all our frustration
and rebellion, we want deeply to be God's people.'

In searching my own experience to try to give them
some hope, I began to see that during these past few
years God had been giving me a new start, a second
touch. As I listened and spoke to this obviously sensitive
and committed young couple, I realized that recently I
had almost forgotten about 'religion'—that instead, I
was thinking about people and God and the problems of

life. I remembered that Paul spoke of our having available the gift of 'the mind of Christ' (1 Corinthians 2: 16). And knowing he did not mean the physical *brains* of Christ, all I could think of was that he was saying that we have available to us the living *perspective* of Christ. Those times when I saw the world through His perspective, although nothing had changed—everything was different. Prayer had meaning again; the Scriptures came alive; and I was drawn out of myself to love other people.

I realized that imperceptibly, as a 'committed Christian', I had very subtly been taught to see the world through a pair of stained glass contact lenses provided, free of charge, by the Christian community. Not only had I become so accustomed to seeing life through those lenses that I didn't know I wore them, but I had issued dozens of pairs to others without realizing it. All were corrected so that the wearer saw the Christian life and lay ministry in terms of predetermined interpretations of the Scriptures and their implications about living modern life. Along with these guidelines came techniques, some of which were helpful in coping with the standard problems of committed Christian living. But after a few years, I found many of these techniques wearing thin and many situations which they did not cover. This dilemma led me to conferences and seminars in a frantic search for new methods and programmes—never questioning the fact that perhaps I needed to take a look at the whole *underlying perspective* through which I had been taught to see the Christian Way to live in this world.

I realized I wanted to try to relive with this couple and with you my own inner struggles as a Christian layman in the Church in trying to build on the foundations of the traditional techniques. I hope that through the writing and reading of these pages God may teach us both something about dealing creatively with the personal problems of 'just living' as insecure—often anxious—men and women, parents, members of His Church.

Chapter 2

MOVING INTO A NEW PERSPECTIVE
HOW DOES ONE CHANGE A VIEWPOINT?

'. . . *he will give you another Counsellor*
to be with you for ever . . .'

John 14: 16 (RSV)

When I made the personal discovery that for me, God is
real, I was all alone on a roadside in East Texas. There
was no one to explain to me that now I was supposed to
be joyous all the time, that to be anxious was sinful, and
that there is a more or less prescribed form in which one
stands up and witnesses for Christ. As a matter of fact, it
was four years after trying to commit my whole future
to God before I ever heard or gave a personal testimony
as such. All I knew was that something had happened to
me which convinced me that God was performing a
revolution in my life. My attention was focused in a new
direction and for the first time as an adult, I felt at home
in His world. For a while, this was enough.

One of the first problems I had was that I could not
find anyone in the Church with whom I could identify
deeply as *a person*. When I would tentatively begin to
talk about a new experience of living, I could see that
people either thought I was naïve or some kind of a religious maniac. I began to feel that my own new commitment to God was different from those of the minister
and many of the leaders in our church, although I could

not explain the difference I felt. I began subtly rejecting them by my questioning and doubting as to the depth of their understanding of the Christian life. Not knowing anyone who seemed to understand what had happened to me, I lived alone inside. I began by trial and error to build a life of prayer, study of the Scriptures and of devotional books. Not having the advantages of a community of people to tell me what to expect as a new Christian, I had to look and decide for myself how a man might live in the modern world, trying to be Christ's person. Those first years were lonely and discouraging in many ways, as I tried to learn to live all over again. I had no group with whom I could test what I was discovering and no one with whose life I could personally identify.

Then, some four years later, I met an old friend who had also (much to his surprise) become converted. But he had been confronted as one of a group, and many of his friends' lives had begun to change at the same time in the same church. I cannot tell you how thrilled I was not to be alone with my new faith. It wasn't long, however, before I realized that my open expressions (of anxiety, for instance) made some of those Christians uneasy. I learned that a 'victorious Christian' should not have some of the problems which I continually faced. I learned that, without seeming to realize it, a number of these people had received Christianity as a sort of 'package deal'. There seemed to be an unpublished list of things which made one more and more acceptable as a Christian. However, notably missing from the list were the very human problems and frustrations which seemed to me to be a natural part of any dynamic and changing life situation. I was a little baffled and felt that there was something unreal about the idea of continual 'unbroken joy' in the midst of vulnerable living. I had not seen this kind of 'tensionless peace' in the lives of Christ, Paul, Augustine, or any of the other spiritual companions of my previous four years. Nevertheless, since these new friends were obviously filled with love of God, and since there were many of them and only one of me, I tried to conform. And I knew a great deal of happiness and release in trying to live for Christ. Yet, as much as I loved these Christians and as much as they taught me, I found that I was lonely and restless inside. I felt that no one understood me; and having a desperate need for approval, I was pretty miserable.

One morning I awoke and said in my prayers, 'God, I have cut off all my audiences—the old oil business crowd, the friends we know socially, the officers of the church, and now this new group of Christians. I don't fit anywhere. No one really seems to appreciate the struggles I have.'

Then, out of the silence, it was as if God said to me, '*I* understand what you are going through. Why don't you play your life to *Me* as your audience? I'll give you the personal consciousness of the acceptance and love you need for your life.'

What a simple thought this appears to be as I write it. Yet, when it really hit me, this idea became a profound turning point for me in trying to live as a Christian—in a world which didn't particularly care whether or not I did. At first I did not understand how deeply this consciously 'playing it to God' could change my life—until I was having a conversation with a friend of ours who was a college football coach. This man's teams had the longest series of wins in the nation. To watch his boys play was sheer joy. They were in superb physical condition, but what impressed me most was their great drive, their motivation to play every minute as if it were the final minute of the game. In practice sessions I remember having the distinct impression that if the coach were to say he wanted six boys to tackle a Greyhound bus, *eight* would have raced to be first. This, I reflected, was not the sort of motivation we had at our church.

Since I was then wrestling with the problem of how to get people motivated to become involved in the church's programme, as well as how I might live for Christ, I went to this friend and asked him to tell me his philosophy concerning football, and I took notes. He told me some fascinating things—that football is basically a 'spiritual' game in that the winner between two teams with nearly equal physical ability is determined by an inner quality of desire to give oneself *totally*. Although this desire is a corporate thing, it must also be deeply individual. I listened to see if I could find out how an individual player on this team might maintain this motivation week after week under the terrific pressure of a long series of wins.

As our conversations continued, I began to see something I had not noticed at first about the boys' performance during games. One of the devices which the coach employed regularly was the use of films for training purposes. On Monday the whole squad, including the coaches, would come in and go over the films, seeing the good and the bad play. In talking to some of the players, I had realized the almost fanatical sense of loyalty and respect many of these boys had for their coach. As I watched the replay of some of the films, I saw that these boys did not seem to be playing the game primarily to the audience in the grandstand. They had a reputation for jumping up after being tackled, running back into the huddle, snapping out, and hitting hard with another move. When the excitement of the game mounted and the crowd grew frantic (the other team often becoming rattled), these boys worked like parts of a well-oiled machine. One day as I watched a game, I understood how this could be. Although the crowd might not know if each boy executed his specific assignment well, the coach would know. Their cool operation would be seen on Monday even if the press had missed it. I thought, *these boys are unconsciously playing the game to a different audience and it has freed them from the frenzy of the crowd!*

I had my answer. Whether or not it was true for the football team it was true for *me!* All of my life I had been influenced too much by the moods of my associates. When they were excited and panicked, I reflected their anxiety. Now, in my new experiment, although I was still performing in the same circles and in the same social and business 'games', I was occasionally finding a calmness and an ability to live with more honesty and integrity than before. I was starting to play my life to a different audience—to the Living Christ.

I wasn't thinking in terms of His 'judging' my actions —but rather of His living *awareness* of my struggles to be His man. I began to get up in the morning being conscious of God's awareness of me and my waking movements. I began being able to tell Him that *He* was the one for whom I wanted to perform the day's actions. Just the conscious act of deciding *that* was a new kind of commitment which, by itself, changed all kinds of things.

Language, for instance. The way I have talked has

always depended, to an amazing degree, on the people to whom I was talking and those within hearing range. There was a semi-conscious editing for the sharpest persons in the group, even with regard to the tone of my voice. If I found myself in a business deal with someone from the deep South, for instance, I might go home with a subtle and unconsciously acquired Southern accent which only Mary Allen would notice. The men I might be with also affected the way I reacted to people. For example, if I were to invite someone whom I respected tremendously to spend the night in our home and to walk through an entire day with me, it would improve my conduct without *any conscious discipline* on my part. While this important person was in our home, I would be a little bit more pleasant about correcting my children (and my wife). I would probably be more attentive to the people who waited on me at the post office or bank.

In retrospect, I realized that I have often been just a little more *Christian* when there was an 'important' Christian with me. And, in this same way, as I consciously attempted to play out my days and hours before a present, attentive Lord, I began to change with regard to my specific consideration of other people. I caught myself saying silently things like, 'Look at this fellow, Lord, he needs You. Help me to know how to love him for You.' This was a private inner process of disciplining myself to cultivate a consciousness of Christ's nearness in every conceivable situation. And this concrete awareness brought about all kinds of subtle changes in my reactions to people and circumstances.

Being conscious of Christ's attention not only affected what I did and said, but what I *saw*. And just seeing people differently changed entire relationships. There was one man, whom I disliked intensely, whose office was close to ours. He was arrogant and a smart aleck; he needled people viciously, many of whom, like the secretaries, could only choke back tears of embarrassment and anger. This man was mad at the world. As an angry smark aleck (which is what I saw when I looked at him), he had no use for Christ's love. But as I began to look at this man, being aware that Christ and I were looking at him together, I began to see—in the same person—a man who was deeply hurt, threatened, and *very* lonely. This is what this man really was inside. It dawned on me that for a man like *that*, Christ's love could have meaning. When I responded naturally to what I now saw as I looked at this man, he began to drop the façade of anger, and the hurt began to come out. Suddenly we were at ease with each other *without anything having been said* to break down the wall. Just by trying to look from Christ's perspective, I saw the real person behind his mask, and somehow he knew and felt loved. I was seeing why the saints had come up with such seemingly simple, basic ways to improve relationships. It was not because they were brilliant. Most of them were not. They had a different perspective; and from that spiritual vantage point, they looked at the unsolvable problems other men saw. However, they saw—in the same situations— different problems. They saw problems which *could* be dealt with through the love and acceptance of God. They saw men as Christ saw them.

I had always vaguely believed that God loved and understood me. But now I was beginning to grasp the notion that God was aware of me and giving me the personal approval I needed to risk changing my attitudes and behaviour. The image of Him, giving me His attention and understanding at each point in my day as I tried hesitantly to be His person, gave me great support. This 'practising the Presence' took a lot of discipline and effort, and I failed pitifully. I would start out in the morning and forget 'to play it to Him' before I got the car started! But each time I realized that I had shut Him out, or each time that I really fouled up and did it my way, I would stop and confess that I loved myself more than Him. And I would start again *right then*.

But, as I usually am, I was terribly impatient. I kept looking for 'results' every day, even though I knew that the lives of the saints have attested that the *real* results are seldom visible to the pilgrim himself. As a matter of fact, instead of saintly results, I began to see the many ways in which my habitual behaviour was *not* God's way. I wanted to change everything right now! In my impatience, I was like the man in Bruner's story who planted a new onion and pulled it up every morning to see if it were growing. I became very discouraged, and then I met the Rev. Ernest Southcott from Leeds, England. I was an intense young Christian and my urgency for changing the Church *today* must have been written across my forehead. After an hour or so of conversation late one night, he asked me, 'Have you ever considered *tunnelling*?'

Tunnelling! I was not sure what he meant, but I did not like the sound of it. When you tunnel, you disappear. I was more of the 'cliff-hanging' type of Christian, clambering up the sheer slate cliff, in my imagination, as I risked failure to find a way over the mountainous obstacles of the faith—shouting back down to my more timid brethren, 'This way, it's all right!' Or, 'Watch out for the sliding rocks here,' as I tried to find a path over the treacherous new ground of our generation's attempt to be God's people. It was as if God were telling me through this man, 'If you ever did make it over the mountain, anyone would have to be a spiritual athlete to follow you; but if you begin now to dig a tunnel, even the crippled ones could make their way.'

Southcott said that he had tunnelled quietly in his parish for five years, trying to learn how to live his faith and to work as a minister, before he had seen any results.[1] Somehow his life told me intuitively that he was right.

I sat down and said to myself: 'I will not look for any results for five years, but will make my life an experiment played out to God alone. I will try to immerse myself and my "actions in relationship" in the perspective of Christ, trying to move into His spiritual vantage point through study, prayer, and involvement with other people.'

What relative freedom! I had never realized that it is the *results* of my actions which have always made me afraid. I had been under pressure to succeed as a provider, parent, husband, and Christian because of the semi-conscious fear that the results of my actions would somehow not be enough. I never knew when I had done or given what I was 'supposed to'. This compulsive doing, because of unseen guilt and insecurity, had come out in some strange ways in my Christian life. For instance, I remember when I had finally developed a regular fifteen minute quiet time of prayer in the mornings, hearing one night at a meeting, a man say he could not get along without *thirty* minutes of prayer a day. I

1. See *The Parish Comes Alive* by Ernest W. Southcott, New York: Morehouse Gorham Co., 1956.

wondered secretly if I were praying 'enough' and if I
should pray more—and compulsively did so.

But after my talk with Ernest Southcott, I was being
freed from comparing myself with other Christians' 'results'. This released me more often to concentrate on
the details *of the tasks and relationships before me,*
instead of on how I was doing as a Christian. I realized
that all my life I had unknowingly let other people's
abilities and experiences intimidate me and cause me to
feel that I was failing.

I remember teaching our little girls to ride a bicycle.
Each one wailed through teary blue eyes, 'Daddy, I'll
never be able to do it. Look, the other girls can ride with
no hands.' I told them to 'forget about the others and
just learn to ride with me holding you'. And one day each
one would realize that I was no longer holding tightly,
and they would have learned. It seemed to me that God
was telling me, 'I'll look after the ultimate effectiveness
of your life, you just learn to go through *today* . . . with
Me holding on . . . and forget about the results and what
the other Christians are accomplishing in their lives.'
By agreeing not to take my spiritual temperature each
day, I stopped thinking so much in terms of doing 'religious' things, I began to relax a little and live; and in
consciously opening my inner stream of awareness and
allowing Christ to be the travelling audience to the
unfolding drama of my insignificant days and nights,
they no longer seem to be insignificant.

It is difficult to describe the intimate sense of discovery I felt in beginning to notice small things around
me. The world was filled with surprising sights I had
always seen, yet never noticed before. If the little ordinary relationships in life could provide the raw

materials for meaning, purpose, and creative fulfilment, then I was beginning to be infinitely wealthy. My life could always be potentially full and growing, whatever my 'success' in the eyes of the world might be—even the Christian world.

One evening last week my eight-year-old daughter was sitting on my lap before the fire. She was crying because she could not remember the eight times tables; particularly that eight times seven equals fifty-six. As I held her and we talked about it, I was aware that this experience with her had taken on a new importance because I was conscious that God was in the room. I realized that the kind of listening patience and love I might have in that private encounter could well be more important, from His perspective, than the way I might speak *about* His love before a thousand people.

This viewpoint quickened my imagination and made me begin to re-examine, with new eyes, the apparently small things in my path which make up my ordinary life. Almost at once I was appalled to find that, even with regard to the Christian disciplines in our home, my vision had been terribly warped. I had not been looking at my family's needs and desires but had subtly been trying to force them into an unreal conformity to the notions of other people. I decided to start my re-examination by looking around at home—to begin to deal with little things—like the children.

Part II

SOME EXAMPLES OF

TRYING TO LIVE IN A NEW

PERSPECTIVE IN CERTAIN AREAS

OF ORDINARY LIVING

Chapter 3

COMMUNICATING A LIVING FAITH TO ONE'S OWN CHILDREN—AN UNCHARTED SEA

'And you shall teach them to your children, talking of them when you are sitting in your house, and when you are walking by the way, and when you lie down, and when you rise.'

Deuteronomy 11: 19 (RSV)

As I have mentioned in another context, my first attempts to live a Christian life in my own home were almost disastrous. I can see now that I had taken my old pre-Christian ideas of what a Christian home ought to be and tried to slowly infiltrate these into our family life. I finally decided to change *myself*, realizing (accurately) that it would be impossible to talk to my wife and children about change in our family unless there was a change in me. So, with much effort, I finally began to get up in the mornings to pray. Mary Allen, however, developed a signal which almost never failed to break my composure, particularly fragile at that time in the morning. I would tiptoe about, ease drawers in and out with great care, then, just as I was leaving the room, she would moan ever so slightly. This moan would let me know, in one incoherent syllable, that (1) I had awakened her and she couldn't go back to sleep and (2) she hoped to goodness I got a lot out of those prayers,

since we were both losing sleep so that I could have my
'quiet time'.

Gritting my teeth, I would go into the den and pray—
usually for patience, which I realized I wouldn't have
needed if I had stayed in bed! Since it is unlikely that
either Jesus or Paul were married, reading in the New
Testament didn't shed too much light on the specific
problems of tunnelling in a house full of family. Yet,
inside I felt almost elated. At last I was *beginning* and,
at first, the obstacles almost made it more of an adventure because it *was* a costly kind of change; it threatened our intimate life together. This change, from a
verbal commitment into an active inner adventure, was
really exciting to me, although, paradoxically, I often
got very little in terms of content out of the quiet times.

Then came the children. My stumbling around early
in the morning must have been very significant to them,
since their earlier memories included games in which
the whole family tried to get Daddy to wake up and to
get out of bed. However, to me, their interest in my
new secret venture was very frustrating. We have three
daughters who, at that time, were about seven, five, and
one. They began, almost at once, to tiptoe quietly in and
crawl on my lap, wanting to know in loud whispers
'what are you doing, Daddy, and why are you reading
that book?' When I stopped and tried to explain to
them, the time was up, and I was late and irritated.
Finally, I remember telling the children one morning
to 'be quiet and get out of here. Daddy's busy!' I will
never forget our middle daughter, sniffling back tears,
asking her mother, through the kitchen door, 'What's the
matter with Daddy?' My wife's matter of fact answer

was, 'Oh, he's learning how to be a good Christian so that he can love the people downtown.'

I was furious! I was also very frustrated. I realized Mary Allen had really hit the truth—and that made it worse. *I was the Christian doing Christian things*, yet it was fouling up my relationship with my own family. My first reaction was, 'Well, they crucified my Lord, too.' But then one day I heard a man say, 'Yes, but don't ever forget, they crucified three that day, and *two* of them deserved it.' The man was right. I saw then that when my family crucifies me, the odds are they may have a point.

One morning a few days later our oldest little girl came in and asked me what I was doing. I stopped reading, put my arm around her, and told her I was trying to learn all I could about Jesus. The Bible was all about Him, and I was reading it and talking to God by praying. She sat with me quietly that morning, and the next. The following week she asked if she could have a Bible. I gave her one, and she began to get up in the mornings with me. Right then I learned something new about communicating at home.

If you want your children to read the Bible and pray someday, get up and do these things yourself—because *you want to*. They'll know if you are really interested or just doing it out of duty. Whether or not they laugh and ignore you, or get up and pray with you, they will remember that it was important to you. Someday when they get ready, they will have a memory of the way you *were* when you got up and whether or not it was automatic or real for you. One of our friends, Charlie Brown, in talking about his time with his children said he had just realized that we parents are in the 'memory-building business'. Memories of us, as we really are, are powerful motivators. I know that, as a young man and even though my father had been dead for many years, when I had an ethical decision to make, I could often see his face in my imagination. I would picture him, facing a similar problem, and thus he helped me in my decisions until I learned to make my own.

Being very encouraged by the new importance small things were having now that I was taking time to notice, I took a new look at my behaviour as a father. Part of my own early training had been that, when I grew up, I should be a 'good father'. When our children came along, and long before my new Christian beginning, I had decided to be a fine dad. Since my own father had been away from home a great deal, I had never been able to get him to play with me very often. I thought *that* must be what a good father would do—play. So, although I knew almost nothing about little girls, I tried to set aside time to play with them. Usually I had other things on my mind and was about half there, but I dutifully tried. As I was beginning to re-examine my role as a father, I remember coming in from work and overhearing one of our children saying to her mother, in a discouraged little voice, 'Mummy, do we *have* to play with daddy to-night?' Oooh!

So, as I had begun to learn to know adults by listening to them, I began to listen to my own children and to try to hear what they were saying, because now they had become important as individuals. As I listened and watched them, individually and specifically, I began to care more about each one in a special way, rather than just 'loving the children'. This did not happen automatic-

ally, or in a week, but over a period of months. I tried
to see them from Christ's perspective (as they really
were) and began to pray about needs in which *they* were
interested instead of just what *I* thought they should
have. I asked questions about the things in *their* world.
Now, they have become personalities I enjoy being with,
although we still fuss and misunderstand each other on
many occasions. Only now it is different, because I have
somehow joined the family. And a funny thing has happened. I had seldom heard the children when they woke
in the middle of the night. Mary Allen could hear them
when they merely rolled over the wrong way in bed—I
could not hear them if they fell out. But as I became
involved with the children as real people, I began to
wake up when they called (and it took me a while to
learn to pretend that *I didn't* . . . but I made it).

I was beginning to see that a Christian father is not
necessarily a playmate. Our daughters often enjoyed
being with me in the garden or while I painted a shelf
much more than when I tried 'to entertain' them. I was
seeing that a father in Christ's perspective might be one
who is *tuned in* to his children, taking each one seriously,
as a person. The time he does have with them would
be spent *really* listening and watching as they try to tell
him something—not always listening with his nose in the
newspaper. I realized that when I had one finger in the
newspaper to keep my place, and was looking question-
ingly at my child, from her perspective I was saying, 'We
have a three minute maximum conversation time.' Actually, it takes less time to put the paper down, hold the
child on your lap and really look at her and listen, especially when she seems to be excited about telling you
something. Then, after responding to what she has said,

and chatting about it, you can tell her that you want to read the paper now. This results in their not being nearly so frantic, because you have held them and heard them and they know it. I believe that fact is more important to them than what they had to tell (and, unless your wife is unduly large, I have found this procedure often works with wives too).

About this time I was speaking to lay groups occasionally and the question began coming up from worried Christian mothers, 'Mr. Miller, what do you do in your home about family devotions?' Well, the truth was that we did not do *anything* about family devotions at our house. But I hated to answer *that*, as the general implication seemed to be that *real* Christian homes had something variously called 'family altar', 'family prayers', or 'family devotions'. This, I found out, was supposed to take place either around the breakfast table with the father reading the Bible or in the evening after supper, during peak TV time—evidently, as the children commented, to make it as painful as possible for the entire family. I began to think about this, and my *conscious* thought at the time was that every Christian family needs such a period of family worship. I had heard this implied or said directly dozens of times by my new Christian friends. Later I saw what really motivated me was the fact that it seemed a real blight on our Christian reputation as a family that we 'didn't love God enough' to have family prayers.

By this time Mary Allen had made a commitment of her life, but her commitment was to Jesus Christ and not to the religious practices of my Christian cronies. When I suggested that we had a family time of Bible reading and prayer, she was willing ,but thought, for us,

it would be unreal. However, one night we tried it anyway. Since my pride was at stake, I was sensitive when
the children complained about it. Our first 'family time'
followed the evening meal. The telephone rang constantly, often for me, so everyone had to wait. Table-
clearing, dishwashing chores, and homework were de-
layed; and we all went to bed tense and cross, but *we
had had our family devotions!* I realized then that it
wasn't Jesus who needed us to have a family altar at our
house, it was Keith. I could see also that each family,
as each individual, has to find the particular 'shape' of its
own life and obedience in terms of its specific situation.
However valuable and important family prayers might
be to other families, it was phoney for us. I recognized
that I had been feeling guilty because I had not con-
formed to other people's ideas about family devotional
life, and I experienced a great sense of relief. I realized
that we would have to try to find other ways and times
to pray which would be meaningful to us.

The following were some of the things which naturally
developed in our family over the years. Both of us have
always said a prayer with each of our children as we
tucked them in at night. We had a standard prayer ritual
of 'now I lay me down to sleep' followed by the 'God-
blesses' (God bless Mummy, Daddy, Sister, Grandma,
the dog next door, etc.). One night as I was going
through this with one of our daughters, I realized that I
wasn't actually praying with my children. I was trying
to teach them to pray instead. It dawned on me that
they had never heard any real confession or petition
from me about things that were *real in my life*. The next
evening I was cross at the dinner table and glowered at
their mother during the meal. That night, as I lay on

our five-year-old middle daughter's bed, I prayed, 'Dear God, forgive me for being cross at dinner tonight.' There followed a kind of awed silence. Then very quickly, she went through the familiar prayer. The next night, 'it just happened', I was also cross during dinner. Again, in my prayers, I said, 'Dear Lord, forgive me for being cross at dinner again tonight and help me not to be so again. I really don't want to be that way. Please help me to try hard not to be.' There was the same silence. Then with eyes clinched shut, my little girl said, 'Dear God, forgive me for weeweeing out in the backyard under the big tree last summer.' I almost laughed and cried at the same time. This was *real* confession at a five-year-old level (of a behaviour which is against the rules at our house).

I saw that, from Christ's perspective, one does not *teach* people to pray; he prays with them out of his own life as Christ did (See Luke 11: 1ff.). They learn by example. Of course, one must pray about things a child can understand and handle emotionally, like happenings around the house or neighbourhood. If you have a seventy-five thousand dollar note due at the bank Monday morning and don't know how you're going to pay it, I would *not* pray about that with a five-year-old. She would have no way of understanding anything about your problem—except possibly the note of terror in your voice. We have fallen into new rituals at our house. But prayer is at least more meaningful than it had been, and some real changes in our lives have come out of this different perspective regarding our prayers at home.

For one thing, I had often wondered what I ought to do about talking to the children regarding Christian commitment, but I didn't want to manipulate them. One night we were having an adult dinner party. I went in to say prayers with our ten-year-old. Being in a state of turmoil about a vocational move I was contemplating, I closed my prayer by saying something like, 'Lord, I want you to take my future and show me what you would like me to do with it. Amen.' My little girl looked up at me very thoughtfully. 'Why did you say that, Daddy?' I looked down at her in surprise, not realizing at once what I had prayed. 'Well,' I replied, 'I'm just trying to give my life to Jesus, honey, so that He can show me the best way to live it.'

'Oh,' she said.

A few minutes later, I was alone in the kitchen when I seemed to feel two little eyes peeking in through a crack in the door. As I looked around, she pushed the door open, came running across the room and threw her arms about my legs. 'What is it, honey?' I asked. She looked up at me thoughtfully. 'Daddy,' she said, 'I'd like to give my life to Jesus, too.'

She had heard the words many times that God loved her and that Christ had died for her. But that night she felt different about them. Right there I explained to her that what *she* was doing was telling God that she wanted Him to be her Lord, that she wanted to get to know Him and love Him, and that she would like Him to show her how to live her whole life for Him. This she did. Now, I don't know what this will mean in her adult life, but it meant something then. And she came to it in the context of her everyday living, hearing us pray sincere prayers out of our real needs.

This is not as easy as it may sound—to begin to be open concerning your own needs, vulnerable in your own home. At first I said to myself: 'If my children see that I am not strong and have to pray for all kinds of strength and help, they won't respect me as a father. I may have some real discipline problems on my hands. Who am I to be telling them to straighten up when I have trouble straightening up myself?'

One day this dilemma came to a head. We were living at an experimental lay conference centre called Laity Lodge. A conference had just been concluded. My wife had been telling some people at our dinner table a story of some experience we had had on a trip. Somewhere in the middle of the story, I deftly took it over—to make sure our friends got the full import of the punch-line. In the process, of course, I squashed Mary Allen and completely took her out of the conversation. Later we exchanges glances, and I realized what I had done. Furthermore, in that instant, I recalled doing this many times before. That night, after the conference members had left, I came into our bedroom and said, 'Honey, I have just realized how I have squashed you by trying to dominate every group we're in . . . and I'm sorry. I don't know if I can do anything about it, but I'm going to try. Please remind me, *very gently*, when I do this so that I can try to stop.'

It has never been easy for me to apologize when I have really meant it, and I had aged a little just getting ready to tell her. When I finished, I noticed that our thirteen-year-old daughter had been standing in the doorway. She looked as though she were feeling miserable at having witnessed this scene and yet hadn't known how to leave. She loves her mother very much. Later that night, as I came in to say prayers with this daughter, she was quiet and a little distant. I realized that I might have alienated her because of her love for Mary Allen. I decided to just go ahead and try to be real in my prayer. After some other prayers, I closed my part by saying something like, 'And Lord, forgive me for squashing mummy by hogging the whole show and not allowing her to be who she is. Help me to be aware of this and not to do it again.' When I had finished, my daughter was looking at me very intently. She looked up and down my face, then hugging me very close, she said, 'Oh, Daddy, I love you so much.'

I learned right there that children already know about our weaknesses. Our faults *show*. And when we refuse to confess them, our children do not think that we're strong, as I had supposed, but that we are either phoney or can't recognize our weaknesses. More generally, I believe they simply learn to imitate us and to keep their own needs hidden and bottled up. I began to realize that unless my children learned from me that they were acceptable to God with all of their incompleteness and missing of the mark (even when they have tried hard to do right), they may never learn it at all. And they will have missed the good news that our acceptance is dependent on God's righteousness and not our own. Of course, I realized that paradoxically we are called to be perfect (Matthew 5: 48), but I am stating that our justification is based on grace, on Christ's integrity and not our own (Romans 3: 23, 24).

We were beginning to learn that, for us, a Christian home didn't feel or sound nearly as 'religious' as we had thought it would. We held hands and prayed at meals, Mary Allen and I both prayed with each child at bed time, and the younger children and I learned to 'talk to God' conversationally, expressing ideas and hopes as well as more conventional prayers. When a crisis has come up in our family, or that of a friend, or a tragedy in the news has touched us, we have sometimes all gathered in our bedroom or around the dining-room table and prayed together, very simply. Sometimes when one of the children, or one of us, is worried, or merely has had a *good* day, we will just hold each other and say, "Thank you, God."

When we first began praying with the children, Mary Allen did not feel at ease praying aloud, so each of us prayed separately with each child. This was certainly not a calculated thing. As a matter of fact, at first I resented it, feeling that her lack of example would be 'bad for the children'. But I have come to realize that the praying alone with the children individually has made for much more intimate and personal involvement in our family. Each child knows that she is going to have a few minutes alone with us separately every evening. We have sometimes shared real joys and pains in these moments. Attending church and Sunday school has been our children's main corporate experience of prayer, except those spontaneous prayers mentioned above and those at meals.

For several years, before bedtime I sometimes read *Hurlbut's Story of the Bible*.[1] On alternate nights I might read children's classics like *Mary Poppins* (before the film came out). Most of the time, Mary Poppins's rating was higher than Jesus', but both led to a closeness as we discussed the people, problems, and humorous happenings in each book. These brief conversations within the family helped us see that all of life is God's

1. J. N. Hurlbut, *Hurlbut's Story of the Bible*, New York: Holt Rinehart and Winston, 1957.

deal. In any case, the important thing I learned is that, by trying to be open to Christ's nearness and to each other and by not forcing each other into a mould, we are learning to live and cope with all of life at home from a new perspective, rather than superimposing religious forms on our life together.

I realize that some of the more traditional observances are natural in some families and that the more structured family devotions may provide a greater sense of family solidarity and may have greater meaning for other families. When this is true, I think it is wonderful. We just happened to find that *for us* the patterns and attitudes I have just described seem more natural. I have come to believe that if a husband and wife are honestly trying to find God's will, the children will somehow get the picture. But I do not *know* about this of course. And in fact it has taken years for me to realize that the way we are trying to live might possibly be as Christian for us as family devotions would have been.

But, as I began to talk to other Christians about what we were learning, these discoveries raised a further question. How much of a risk was I willing to take to try to learn how I should live for God? The Chrstian community might not approve of my discoveries and the ways I was trying to live in Christ's perspective. New ways do not sound the same as the old and therefore may be threatening to the security of some who are using the tried methods. Besides, I might be wrong. How was I going to face the subtle criticism that I was not being a 'consistent Christian' and yet still be free to live creatively in Christ's will as I could determine it?

Chapter 4

A LOOK AT CHRISTIAN CONSISTENCY

'. . . when they measure themselves by one another, and compare themselves with one another, they are without understanding.'

II Corinthians 10: 12 (RSV)

Dr. Paul Tournier writes about a time when he was listening to a prominent medical authority speak and hearing the man come out with this statement:

Neurotics, he said, are people who cannot say d——*. This very unacademic word sounded well in that scholarly assembly, and in its terseness expressed a penetrating truth, namely that, sooner or later, in order to fulfil his destiny in the way God has planned, every man must brave the judgment of others, even that of his parents, his masters, and perhaps of the religious authorities, . . .[1]

I was finding that in my own home, when and if I was willing to risk it, God was showing me ways of looking at life and relating to people which were changing the whole experience of living for me. But often these new insights did not fit the Christian community's established picture of a consistent Christian life. I was continually

* Dr. Tournier's deletion.

1. Paul Tournier, *Guilt and Grace*, New York: Harper and Row, 1962, p. 70.

surprised to discover how stereotyped my preconceived ideas had been about how one should live and solve problems as a Christian. Instead of looking at a new problem creatively, as I would in business, I would look at problems in my personal relationships and try to 'remember' the Christian solution from the Scriptures or Christian reading. So instead of really being engaged in the anguish of the moment with the person before me, my mental attention would often be back in the Scriptural memory library of my mind, thumbing through passages looking for 'the truth'.[2] Don't misunderstand me. I read the Bible regularly and have for years and am trying to immerse myself in its truth. I have committed many passages to memory and find them very helpful. But I realized that my desire to be a consistent Christian with correct Christian answers was making me into a modern version of the Pharisee in a natural shouldered suit. I was thinking so much about my helpful answers that I wasn't hearing the real questions or entering into the *problems* people had. I was feeling more secure in my own knowledge about the faith and tended to over-simplify the way God helps people—conveniently (but actually) forgetting my own agonizing times. Somehow I had evidently got the signal from the Christian group that the valleys and hills in my life should be straightened out by now. And when I talked

2. Now even to say this sounds as if I am implying that there are 'better' answers than those found in the Scriptures. But that is *not* what I am saying. I think a sound New Testament approach is to immerse yourself in the Scriptures in private and then *focus your attention on the people and the current situation creatively*. God will still be around to provide some good words, even in some pretty important situations. (See Matthew 10:18-20, Mark 13:11.)

with other Christians about this, I discovered that 'consistency' is considered to be one of the most important and desired characteristics of living the Christian life. I was spiritually sick because the more I was living in what I thought was Christ's perspective on this adventure of faith, in one sense the more *inconsistent* my behaviour seemed to be—according to some evangelical teaching about how to live and witness. Being very insecure I would go back and try to conform.

I was pretty discouraged and confused. But then I saw a surprising thing in reading the New Testament. Whereas I had always blindly assumed that Christ was very consistent in His life, I saw suddenly that He was *not*. In fact, Jesus was very *inconsistent* in His life! And it was His inconsistency, according to the religious habits of His day, which kept Him in hot water and eventually led to His death. For example, on one hand He said that He had not come to change even the smallest punctuation mark of the Jewish law (Matthew 5: 17 ff), and then He proceeded to break their sacred rules one after the other—even on the Sabbath—to love the people from His Father's perspective in obedience to Him (Mark 2: 15–17, 18–22, 23–28; 3: 1–5). He told His followers not to use physical violence to conquer the world; in fact, He told them that they should turn the other cheek (Matthew 5: 39). But in a later situation we see a furious Jesus, driving employees out of the Temple and throwing over their stalls (Matthew 21: 12). Or on another occasion we see Him telling a group of scribes and Pharisees that they were rotten inside (Matthew 23: 27–28). Then a few days or weeks later, He died for them. These are just a few of the acts of a Man who was notoriously *inconsistent*. Why did He behave that way?

As I thought about this, I knew I was on the track of something very important if I was ever going to see life in Christ's perspective.

So I began to examine my old ideas about consistency and I realized that in my insecurity, I had unconsciously assumed that *consistency* in Christian living meant *uniformity*—that we were all supposed to act *alike* and to respond the *same* way all the time. I suppose I had assumed that what God is doing is recruiting a sort of 'spiritual trumpet corps', each member like the next one ethically and morally, and in order to be consistent with our own group, we begin to take on a conformity to its 'sound'. We witness and pray alike. We see at which angle we are to hold the trumpet and when we are to pick it up and put it down. I have found that I can listen to a man either preach or pray and tell you (a good many times out of ten) in what denomination he was trained or even the interdenominational group through which he got converted—by the *sound* of his language, which is usually unconscious to him. Baptists have a different 'sound' from Presbyterians for instance, they use different names for God when they pray, etc. The 'God is dead' and social action groups each have their own pet phrases and identifying words—their own sounds, and when I went outside our church to hear men speak in other denominations, I found that I wasn't really listening to Christian speakers' *thoughts*, I was *first* listening to see if they had 'our sound', and if they didn't, I switched off. Haven't you ever turned on the radio and heard a panting, frantic, haranguing preacher and switched him off without really hearing *anything* he might have to *say*—because he didn't have your sound? I think in my unconscious desire for consistency with *our group* I have switched off

some people who might really have helped me to wholeness in Christ; I let an artificial barrier separate me from
part of Christ's body. But the new discovery to me is that
the Christian Church is *not* a trumpet corps—but an
orchestra—that we are not all *supposed* to sound alike
because *each of us is a different shaped instrument*. God
has given us *our own* individual sounds, our own lives.
For years I have been a piccolo trying to play in the tuba
section, because some men I admire greatly play the
spiritual 'deep notes'. Can you imagine anything more
pitiful than a piccolo trying to play in the tuba section?
Yet this is the story of much of my life, and I had never
felt free and natural in my Christian living because I had
always tried to be something I was not, so that I could be
'like a child of God' (like those *other* children of God
around me).

Where then had this idea come from that Jesus lived
a consistent life and, therefore, we ought to also? Then I
knew. Jesus was not consistent with regard to a set of
rules.[3] He lived out His days in consistent obedience to
a Living Creative Composer, who was composing a
masterpiece of lives and giving Jesus His part in it to
play, a line, an hour at a time, as He listened and watched
in His life. To be obedient to the perspective of His
Father in new situations, Jesus transcended the old rules.
He tried to bring God's vulnerable but healing love to
each situation in a way that brought *wholeness to the
people involved*, however inconsistent His behaviour

3. I am not talking about the ten commandments, which Jesus
did obey of course. But with regard to men's relationships he and
Paul both tried to summarize all these laws into a *perspective of
love* to avoid the kind of legalism of which I am speaking.
(Matthew 22:37ff., Romans 13:9ff.)

might seem to the secular mind or even to the Jewish keepers of the truth and defenders of the faith.

But Jesus' consistency was to a perspective of loving obedience. This has always made Him and His way very threatening, especially to religious people, because we cannot control this kind of life in others. And if we try to live it, we must take the risk of being considered un-righteous by our religious peers. Being misunderstood about our faith and accused of self-centred motives or 'lack of discipline', etc., is hard for a sensitive Christian to take. Some religious leaders have always thought people who talk about this kind of creative freedom from consistency are talking about a kind of irrespon-sible licence, a kind of freedom from discipline and re-sponsibility. But, of course, this is *not* true. As a matter of fact, I am finding that trying to discover and live creatively in Christ's perspective is far more demanding in terms of prayer and study of the Scriptures and risk-ing, than it was to follow the standard little personal habits and rules outlined by our part of the Christian community. This is not speaking against personal or cor-porate disciplines. *Quite the contrary.* In my own life I find that time alone each day in prayer, reading of the Bible and devotional classics, and public worship are a continuing necessity. It is the practice of these disciplines which, in fact, acts as a valuable check against a rootless subjectivism.

So, it seemed to me that if it were true that each of us was to find the particular creative form of his own obedi-ence, then it was *all right* for me to be a piccolo. I did not have to pretend that I was a tuba. What a relief! I saw that I had always been living a life like a suit two sizes too large, sort of hoping I would grow into it. I had felt so insecure inside about my ability to live up to the image I had set as a model for myself that I had never felt at home in my own skin. I once heard a friend say that he had taken the most outstanding characteristic or ability of each of the greatest Christians he had known and built for himself a composite picture of a Christian —and then tried to live up to the *whole thing*. And I realized I had done the same thing. I had taken C. S. Lewis's ability with the written word in English, Elton Trueblood's discipline, Gert Behanna's sheer emotional power as a person on the platform, Sam Shoemaker's ability in helping people individually to find a handle to the doorway into the kingdom—all these and many more. Unconsciously I was trying to be *all* of these things, and, needless to say, I wasn't succeeding and felt discouraged. But now I was discovering that I could just *be me*, for Christ's sake. As a matter of fact, that is the only way I can play my true part in the orchestra. When I really believed this, I set out to try to live a life-sized life.

My first discovery was that I didn't have the slightest notion of how to be my real self. I didn't even know my true abilities. In some segments of our society in America one is considered a shirker if he isn't driving himself to greater things. Especially in some groups of Christians; one has to have made a new discovery, led someone else to a deeper commitment, taken part in a demonstration, or read the latest book when he sees his old Christian friends—or he doesn't feel 'with it'. And having been accustomed to think this way, I was afraid if I relaxed any of my efforts I'd get lazy, or fail, or both.

But being a compulsive worker and doing twice the number of things I could normally handle, what I needed to do to live a realistic life for Christ was to *cut down* on the 'Christian activities' in which I was engaged. Finally, as in the case of those other changes I had begun, which eventually seemed to have been made from God's perspective, I had to specifically bite off a very small piece of life to work on. This is a principle I seem to have to learn again and again: that Jesus started people out with very mundane specific acts (see Matthew 8: 4, Mark 3: 5, Luke 5: 24, etc.), and He tried to get His disciples to concentrate on the present moment with the challenges of each day (Matthew 6: 34).

Secular psychology has had to learn the hard way that little things have vast significance. Sigmund Freud became convinced that small errors had deeper causes and that dreams had definite meaning. Yet scientists poohpoohed him because small errors weren't worthy of examination and dreams had been important to primitives in a magical way. So, scientists could not believe that these little things might provide keys to unlock men's unconscious lives. Yet millions have been led to new understanding and release in life because of Freud's studies.[4]

I am certainly not trying to slip Freud into the Christian community. I disagree with him profoundly in many areas—particularly with regard to his views about God. But I believe that certain efforts concerning church renewal have suffered from the same basic weakness that pre-Freudian psychology had. The Church has for so long searched for *big* organizational answers to its problems that it has often overlooked the broad importance

4. Sigmund Freud, *A General Introduction to Psychoanalysis*, New York: Washington Square Press, Inc., 1962. See p. 88f.

of very intimate personal issues like some of those we
are discussing. Part of this neglect has been a justified reaction against an 'uninvolved pietism'. But a lack of
perspective on some of these small earthbound matters
has blocked great and insignificant men alike in their
attempts to live for Christ. I have come to believe that
we may have ignored the keyhole of being personally
specific in our attempts to batter down the door with
programmes to get to 'renewal'. I feel that the real potential strength and freshness for the Church corporately
will centre around the God-given perspective and insight
of its leaders. But to be relevant to the laymen in the
church *before* these things can be expressed with integrity
in *corporate* action that perspective and insight must be
translatable into daily acts of obedience and surrender
of the will of the individual in real life situations. In any
case, I was finding that the problem before me was to
learn how to live a natural sized *day* in Christ's perspective, before I could begin to tell other men about a
natural sized *life*.

Chapter 5

A NEW PLAN—LEARNING TO LIVE IN MY PART OF THE JUNGLE

'I do not pray that thou shouldst take them out of the world . . .'

John 17: 15 (RSV)

Living in the moving thicket of a commuter's life, I suppose I had been searching for a mighty plan to mow down the seemingly unchristian complexity of the vocational jungle for Christ's sake. But now I set out one morning to see if I could learn to *live*, to simply be myself as God had made me. I wanted to operate within my emotional income. This meant that I would have to learn to live as an average, aggressive lay businessman, walking along the insignificant paths on which my own life in the city took me, day in and day out. I wanted to see this life of mine as Christ saw His, walking along the paths He took in Nazareth. I wanted to see my life from His perspective. If He had not been bored with the commonplace things of life, who was I to demand ever more exciting and scintillating companions, challenges, and experiences in order to be happy as a Christian. But I did not know how to begin living naturally. Finally I decided to go through a whole day trying consciously to see what I was *actually doing* to love the people with whom God had put me. It was quite a day.

On the way to work I stopped for petrol at the service

station I had been patronizing for several years. The attendant smiled and said, 'Good morning, Mr. Miller.' I was sort of shocked as I realized that I had seen this man dozens of times and yet had never really *noticed* him as a person. He knew my name, and I didn't have the vaguest idea what his was. And *I* was the Christian witness. I saw that this man was a person to whom God had introduced me to love for Him. Glancing quickly at the name tag on his uniform, I said, 'Good morning, Charlie.' After he had serviced the car and I was signing the credit card receipt, I tried to think of some natural thing to say to a man whom I had ignored for three years to let him know I was interested in him as a person. Because suddenly I *was*. I finally came out with, 'I say, Charlie, do you have a family?'

He stopped and looked at me a second. When he saw that I really seemed to want to know, his smile spread clear across his face. 'Do I have a family?' And he pulled out his wallet with pictures of about nine children. This was the beginning of a new relationship which soon became a first name friendship with Charlie. One of his children later got seriously injured in an accident. When I read about it in the paper, I knew who it was and could go and find out what might be done, not as a 'Christmas hamper Christian' but as a friend—because we were already friends at the station.

But that first morning after I left Charlie I drove on to my office downtown and went into the indoor car park. The same thing happened, 'Good morning, Mr. Miller,' only this time I was more relaxed and found out that Al had a family too (all this in a few minutes without keeping him from his work). I was discovering that if one is

really interested, he can soon find out a great deal
about people—in a few minutes a day.

Men and women seemed to come out of the wood-
work that day in the First National Building where my
office was, people I had never really seen as *persons*: the
old gentleman who ran the elevator, the secretaries in
the office, the bank teller, the head waiter at the Petro-
leum Club. Although I could not speak to them all that
day, I found that just a question, an interested ear, and
one might create a 'thirty-second island' of caring in a
person's otherwise impersonal day. In the months to
come I saw these sketchy outlines develop into the foundations of some real relationships for Christ and for me.

For years I had been trying to witness to those I considered to be 'important', and the people along my
daily path might as well have been trees walking by me.
It was as if I were opening my eyes for the first time and
seeing the world of the present moment. I was finding a
life-sized life at last—a life that wasn't so far beyond my
ability that it left me continually frustrated, exhausted,
or guilty. I began to realize, emotionally as well as intellectually, that I was discovering a way to live out my
days in the business world in a new relationship with
God's people, a way which was making it possible for
me to find reality in simple day by day contacts, since I
now felt that these had significance for God.

I had thought before that I had to be a big churchman to do big things for God. Consequently most of my
'Christian work' was frustrating and left me miserable,
because its success depended on my manipulating other
people into my programme. But as I looked around me
and found the people and work in my own world to be
real, I began to feel more and more the sense of being on

a secret mission of faith for Christ. I was creatively trying to learn how to love people on their terms and to
pray for them. Occasionally, there were some disap-
pointments and rejections. Some people have forgotten
how to respond to the personal in life. My motives were
occasionally misunderstood—and were bad sometimes.
I don't know what my beginning to see *persons* did for the
people I knew, but it certainly changed me. I had a sense
of 'having time' for people and the exciting feeling of
being on 'new ground', on which I was not just imitating
the most outstanding Christians I knew.

The focus of life was almost imperceptibly changing
from the distant horizon of tomorrow or next month to
the immediate present, the *now*. I saw that so much of
my life had been spent in a world of unreality. I was
either regretting (or at least reliving) incidents and relationships in my past, or I was envisaging great con-
quests or possible tragedies in the future. Now I can see
that the past is only a dream. I cannot affect it or change
it. It is no longer changeable. And the future is equally
unreal, since it does not yet even exist. As a matter of
fact I realized that the only *real* time there is, or ever has
been in which to live and act, is the now—the present
moment.[1] No decision, no birth, no death, nothing ever
happened in a future or a past moment, only in a present one. And I had filled so many of the present
moments of my life with the unreality of the past or
future. The blinding introspection in which I had spent
so much time had again and again blurred the intensity
of my attention from seeing the *actual* opportunities

1. I am indebted to Howard Butt for bringing this idea forcibly
to my attention in a talk to a conference group at Laity Lodge.

and relationships which stood waiting before my eyes. I had marched into the future looking straight ahead—passing by the unconsciously searching eyes of those people beside the road which I was travelling.

This simple change of the focus of my attention to the immediate events of the moment as the important events —from God's perspective—made me realize that all of my background and training were not a kind of 'practising' preparing me for some big public Christian position sometime in the future. (I used to wonder 'what all this hell is training me for?') I now began to see that all my past was training me for the events and encounters of this *day*, however insignificant this day may seem from my perspective. Each day, each relationship, in my business life began to take on new importance. God might have something new to do in *this* relationship. I saw in the Scriptures that the days on which Christ was born, crucified, and rose from the dead did *not* seem important *as they were happening* even to most of the people present, but *only* to those who saw the events of those days from God's perspective. I began to realize that I could easily miss out on the things God may be doing in *this* day—the seeds He is planting, the new visions of renewal, the despair He wants to heal, the hope He wants to fulfil in a life—unless I began to see the possibilities of His healing action all around me along the pathways He will send me *this hour*.

In a way, this may sound easy, but it is *not*. The discipline of living in the now is the most difficult I know; I fail constantly, sometimes for weeks. But paradoxically, there is real power in this sort of living. The people who give themselves to the present moment are also giving themselves more wholly to the people they are with at that moment. If you and I are together, and I am un-consciously glancing at my watch, fretting about the next hour or appointment or later event, *you* are going to be less open than if you have my complete attention *right now*. *You* experience my lack of attention as a lack of interest in *you*. So, almost automatically by living in the present, every relationship is potentially more real, is potentially more life-changing. Also, if I think of *this* as the important moment in our relationship, I find that I am not quite as likely to manipulate you now or butter you up in order that you may do something for me in the future. For I am trying to hear and deal with the mean-ing of what you are saying and doing now. Whereas when my focus of attention is on future goals, however noble, my present words and actions toward you are al-most always edited toward shaping your opinion or ac-tion for the accomplishment of my goal later.

Also, as I have listened and watched people who seem to be alive to the present situation in which they find themselves, I have discovered a profound experience of 'life' or 'presence' when I am with them. This is true whether the person is an actor on the Broadway stage or a teacher working with tough Christian businessmen. This sort of aliveness is winsome and makes me more alive as I respond to the Life I see in them. It draws me toward that Life. It is as if our attention were a powerful spot-light, the beam of which God lets us direct. We can shine this beam off into the past or future or into the eyes of the people around us in the present. When people focus their interest deeply into my life, something happens be-tween us—we move into the warmer arena of the per-sonal—the situation changes, and I am suddenly alive with them . . . I began to see that *agape* love rides down the beam of our attention into people's hearts. And I think that this basic attention to individuals in the present moment may be the greatest kind of love we can give them. For in a strange way we are giving them our lives in that instant, when we are giving them our whole attention. I have come to believe that this is perhaps the most real way to value a person as a human being—to really be *with* him and take him seriously as he is. A single such contact may change the whole direction of a life, a single experience of helping someone realize that he is really of some value.

Last year a girl came several hundreds of miles to a conference I was also attending at Laity Lodge. In a small group we were talking about the people who had had the greatest influence in our lives. The last person to speak was this very attractive young woman in her twenties. She told us that when she was about twelve years old, Elton Trueblood was speaking in the city in which she lived. He was staying in her parents' home. She told us that during the day or two he was there, he talked to her, asked her questions, and listened to what *she* had to say, just as he did to her parents. She said that although he never knew it, that brief experience as a young girl of being taken as an authentic, intelligent Christian had made her want deeply to be one, and had changed the direction of her life.

I suppose what I am saying is that in trying to find a way to live a simple, natural life for Christ in the midst of the action of common living, I am finding that what I have always thought of as the *process*, the daily living, has become the *end*. It is as if God has adjusted the lenses of my eyes so that people and objects in the present, which had been blurred and indistinct as I stared towards the horizon, have taken on a new sharpness and reality. And because the present has become absorbing, I no longer feel the haunting need to get *further on* to some undefined something in my Christian life in the future. I am learning to turn again and again to the Lord of the present moment to find the eternal quality of life of which Christ spoke (John 17: 3).

Not long ago I heard a story which helped me see again the paradoxical power in living in the *Now*. Several years ago a very busy business executive was rushing to catch a train. He had almost given up trying to live a 'personal' daily life because of the great demands on his time—speaking engagements and administrative duties in his organization. This particular morning en route to Grand Central Station he promised himself that he would try to *be* a Christian that day instead of only talking about it. By the time he had picked up his ticket, he was late. Charging across the lobby and down the ramp with his bags, he heard the last 'all aboard'. He was about to get on the train when he bumped into a small child with his suitcase. The little boy had been carrying a new jigsaw puzzle, the pieces of which were now scattered all over the platform.

The executive paused, saw the child in tears, and with an inward sigh, stopped, smiled and helped the boy pick up his puzzle, as the train pulled out.

The child watched him intently. When they finished picking up all the pieces, the little boy looked at the man with a kind of awe. 'Mr.,' he said hesitantly, 'are you *Jesus?*'

And, the man realized that for the moment—on that platform—he had been.

Chapter 6

CHRISTIAN *RESTLESSNESS AND ANXIETY*

'. . . *In the world ye shall have tribulation . . .*'
John 16: 33 (AV)

Almost from the beginning of my introduction into the fellowship of Christians, I can remember hearing people imply or say outright that *restlessness, anxiety,* and *incompleteness* were signs of the non-Christian life and that *peace, security,* and *completeness*, were signs of the Christian life. When I found out that anxiety and incompleteness were thought to represent evidences of sin and evil, I started feeling unacceptable at any time I was not consciously joyful. Then one day I woke up anxious, afraid, and feeling very insecure—all adding up to a frightening loneliness and doubt about the reality of my Christian commitment—just when I had seemed to be getting my Christian life under control.

Thinking that this experience was a sign of evil infiltrating my life, I redoubled my spiritual efforts: more attention to prayers and Scripture reading, etc. And these things helped awhile. But sometimes they did not. Since I felt that anxiety was sinful, I began semi-consciously to feel guilty about it. This only caused more anxiety. The more I looked within myself, the more withdrawn I became. I did not want to get out and witness about a joyful life when I was miserable inside. Further, I hated to admit it, but my Christian friends began to get on my nerves. They *seemed* so untroubled, and I knew intuitively that some of them *must* have similar problems. So I started faking it again, without even being conscious of it. Someone would call and say, 'Hullo there, how are you feeling?' And I would reply, 'Fine, things couldn't be going better,' when in reality I was worried sick. Don't misunderstand, I am not suggesting you tell everyone about your every ache and pain in order to be scrupulously honest, but we Christians have begun to feel as if it is a denial of Christ to be miserable. Consequently most of our friends, being human, are left alone and guilty in their times of misery. But I began to see that this position of hiding our humanity is that of the 'whitewashed sepulchres', smiling on the outside and rotten with guilt, anxiety, and incompleteness within. I knew all this intellectually, but I caught myself hiding my misery also. My conscious reason was that revealing my feelings of need would harm other people's faith. In retrospect I realize that I was really afraid that people might think *I* was not truly committed, or I wouldn't have these feelings. As I struggled with this problem, I had to take a new look at my human nature—the human nature of a man who wanted with all his heart to be God's person and yet found himself anxious and restless inside. Why should *I* have vague feelings of dependency and incompleteness, just when I seemed to be living a disciplined, outgoing life?

In studying psychology and some existentialist literature, I had often read that religion is only a phase, not only historically but in each man's pilgrimage toward maturity and wholeness. In my anxiety I had the sobering thought that maybe I was about to 'outgrow' Christianity, as some of my psychologist friends thought I would . . . or should. I remember being struck particularly by Erich Fromm's conviction that a mature man comes finally to the point at which he internalizes the idea of God to the extent that he no longer speaks of Him and He becomes only a symbol.[1] According to this line of reasoning, those of us who continue to *really need* God are only revealing deep dependency needs. The notion these men present is that hopefully we can outgrow these profound but immature needs, and with them, the need for God.

As a Christian, I have often just shaken my head and tried to ignore the troublesome problems these men suggest. But my own existential anxiety was driving me to take a new look. As I read the Scriptures along with psychological studies on anxiety and dependency, I began to see that Christianity *does* account for these deep needs. Man seems to be *born* with a deep disequilibrium and incompleteness (or dependency need) just as physically he is born with built-in recurring hungers for food and sex. It is the activity of these physical needs which forces each child to communicate with the world and shapes his relationships and communicating habits. A baby's hunger makes him scream, and at that moment his verbal communication with the world has begun. And I think there are psychological needs as deeply given in the human situation as physical hunger.[2] The deep-seated 'dependency' need of which I am speaking is

1. Erich Fromm, *The Art of Loving*, New York: Bantam Books, 1963. See Chapter II, especially pp. 53–69.

2. For a brief discussion of one group's experimental attempts to understand 'exploratory behaviour'—man's motivation from *within* to search for knowledge about life—see Daniel E. Berlyne, 'Curiosity and Exploration', *Science*, 1966 (July 1) Vol. 153, pp. 25–33.

experienced as a vague indefinable restlessness, a need for attention, or for success, or fame, or love—one is not sure what. And this motivating incompleteness keeps us from being *independent* from the rest of the world, so that whatever specific forms it takes, it *is* a deep dependency need. It drives us from one success or failure to another, from one woman to another, from one philosophy or psychology to another. We are drawn ever onward to different challenges, different people, different spokesmen as we search almost frantically for something, or someone to quiet our restlessness.

As Christians, we have realized that this universal existential need is a *built-in* or instinctive need for God and other people, which will not let man rest short of the deep completion and relatedness for which he was made. It was this sense of relatedness which I was realizing in my new relationship with Christ and with people around me. At a profound level I knew the *big* search for meaning and security was over, even though I still had uncertain and unsettled times. As Augustine described this universal dependency need in Christian terms: 'Thou madest us for Thyself, and our heart is restless, until it repose in Thee.'[3]

In wrestling with my anxiety as a Christian, I saw that this restless desire which drives us to God causes a great deal of our anxiety as human beings. There is a fear that our deepest need will not be met. In fact some people have told me in anguish that they were afraid to *really* commit their lives to God for fear that He would not be real, and *then* what would they do. So they 'keep Him alive' by keeping their distance, since they could

3. *The Confessions of St. Augustine*, New York: E. P. Dutton and Company, Inc., 1951, p. 1.

not endure a world without the hope, however remote, that their deepest and most haunting needs would be met. Since the relationship with God and with His people has begun to fill this deepest existential vacuum for millions of men and women, many people in the church have unconsciously assumed that when one truly begins the Christian life, the anxiety should disappear forever, and that its presence after conversion is a sign of a relative falling back into an uncommitted state.

But now I was finding that *we do not throw off this deep need* just because we become Christians. In fact, this drive is the *recurring* hunger that now forces us to *grow* as Christians. When I accepted Christ as Lord and Saviour (from the hopeless quest of living without God), this deepest need in my life was arrested. I felt free from the frantic nature of the basic 'drivenness' of life. Having a great purpose now, I set out to live this life through the disciplines which seemed to go along with it. But then, when I began to conquer the disciplines, I started unconsciously not to depend on God and His people but on my acquired knowledge *about* these things. My dependence was once again in my ability; only this time in my religious ability, and not in the strengthening love and power of God. Getting to be known by a few Christians, *I* was being depended on and felt that I must be religious and strong, not anxious and weak — when the truth is that I often *am* anxious and weak. But I had subtly put myself in God's place again, to be for other people that which they needed—God. But *He* is the only One who can meet our basic dependency needs. He designed them. And I had become anxious and incomplete again because I had conquered the techniques and was unconsciously on the hunt once more for

a deeper security than they provided. At last this search
sent me to my knees as a child, beginning again. It was
my anxious sense of incompleteness which God had used
to drive me back to the place where I would again put my
life in His hands. For me then, Christian restlessness was
not *necessarily* bad, but, like physical pain, it could be a
warning signal—warning me that something was over-
loaded in my life, that something was out of balance.
And because of the signal which anxiety provided, I
could stop and do something before I destroyed myself.

When I realized that man's existential sense of dependency and his periodic anxious restlessness are a part
of the fabric of Christian living, I was quietly awed. Instead of driving me away from Christianity, as this discovery has some of my 'God is dead' (or seriously
wounded) friends, I was thrilled. Because this discovery—that my restlessness is there to get my attention
and point me back toward Christ—freed me as I have
never been freed to *be human* as a Christian. If my faith
is in *God*, then my job is not to build a successful, un-
tainted religious life; it is to live a joyous and creative
human life. I am to love Him, love His people and love
living—poor and incomplete as I am or ever will be—
yet free not to have to be a God-shaped wooden saint.
My recurring restlessness is a natural part of life, driving
me ever deeper in my relationship with Him. I found that
the more my ultimate trust was in God, the *less* I tended
to be involved in *neurotic* dependency relationships with
people. And I saw how Jesus could live trustingly among
men but not lay the burden of His *primary* trust on them,
knowing they could not fulfil it (John 2: 24). And in
some way which I could not understand, the more ulti-
mately I was dependent on God and not ashamed to be

weak, the more power I seemed to have to help people.

At about the time I was wrestling with this matter of inner weakness, I remember being asked to speak to a men's group on the subject, 'The Christian Life'. I went to the meeting and spent five or ten minutes telling the men very honestly that I was feeling miserable. I was tired of speaking to groups and of being a Christian, and had even considered not coming that night. Then I told them that I had thought about my life that day. I had realized that whatever else had had meaning to me besides Christ was so far back in second place that I had decided to come and tell them that I was a Christian almost by default. I had come to the meeting on the chance that some of them might be living with misery and incompleteness too—that some of them might be looking for a Way which could give purpose and meaning even to restlessness and its accompanying despair in themselves. I had thought that my honest and specific confession of my miserable restlessness and self-centredness would force these men to reject me and any message I might have to give them. Instead, I found a room full of brothers, of warm, struggling fellow human beings, who also needed a second touch from our Lord, even though many had been committed Christian ministers for years.

As I thought about the power of that experience of simply being human with those men, yet a professing Christian, I took a look at the New Testament. I saw that Paul had some very anxious, despairing moments, being 'so utterly unbearably crushed that we despaired of life itself' (2 Corinthians 1: 8). J. B. Phillips, the New Testament translator, in discussing this matter points out the fact that as Christians 'we can be overcome by the

most terrifying darkness and reduced to a sense of inadequacy amounting to near desperation.'[4] He goes on
to say that 'the stiff upper lip business is not necessarily
Christian; it sounds much more like a throwback to the
Stoics than to early Christianity . . . The letters (of Paul)
tell no story of idealized human beings but reflect the
lives of people who are changed but by no means perfect.'[5] I was understanding, finally, that the burden of
being happy for Christ was not mine. I was free to own
my true feelings on any given day—without denying
Christ.

Some people in the church today are talking about a
'totally committed' state in which one is forever de-
livered from restlessness or anxiety. But when I talk with
such people or when I read about the life of 'total and
continual peace' in a devotional book, I try to see what
the author's *life situation* was like. In a number of cases
the totally trouble-free Christian person, although perhaps resigned to material poverty, has in some way in-
sulated himself psychologically from any future severe
change in his material responsibility in the world. Some
have joined monastic orders, some have flung themselves
on the world 'to let God provide'. This latter course may
seem to require the greatest kind of courage, and in
many cases it may; but having tried it in one sense, it
also *can be* a real abdication from responsibility. As to
security, I have never heard of such a person starving in
our society. Some 'totally peaceful' Christians have had
enough materially from secure jobs and are content to
keep these jobs and minister in them. Some have been

4. J. B. Phillips, *The Ring of Truth*, New York: The Macmillan Company, 1967, p. 64.
5. *Ibid.*, p. 65.

housewives who have had good providers. I am grateful that people can be freed to live for Christ, unencumbered by the threat of the competitive material world. I think, as a Christian, one might—within the walls of such a situation—avoid existential anxiety and restlessness, perhaps almost indefinitely in some cases. But when a man becomes *genuinely psychologically vulnerable* in the world, I believe he *will* have anxious moments. I do not think these anxious moments are evil or that they necessarily indicate a lack of Christian courage. As a matter of fact, if one is *not* afraid in truly threatening circumstances, then Christian courage is a mockery.

We get the idea that to be courageous is to be totally unafraid and not anxious in the face of real danger. Most fear is a natural reflex action to a genuine threat to one's life or well-being. Healthy people have it. It goes along with the instinct of self-preservation. One who is not conscious of any fear in a genuinely threatening situation is seldom heroic. He is more likely to be grossly insensitive or out of touch with reality. I have come to believe that Christian courage consists in *seeing the danger fully*, reacting to it with human finiteness and fear, and *yet* being willing to face the dangerous situation for Christ or for a brother, through God's support. God did not say He would take us out of the humanness of the world. He said that He loves us and will be with us and that through faith we can overcome that human weakness and can act with courage *in spite of* it. So, although we still experience fear, God has given us a 'cure' for it— an overriding trust in the love of God.[6] Paradoxically, it is the experience of fear and restlessness which brings

6. See *The Life and Letters of Father Andrew*, edited by Kathleen E. Burne, London: A. R. Mowbray Co. Ltd., 1961, p. 252.

back a recurrence of the personal realization of one's humanness, and a new commitment encounter with the living God, at increasingly deeper and more subtle levels of awareness about life.

Many psychologists have found that recurring times of human restlessness seem to cluster around certain crises or stages in every person's life cycle. Erik Erikson of Harvard has postulated eight stages of man's development which represent distinct crises in life.[7] If this is true, then there are certain times in the life of every man (Christian or not) when the very threat of moving into a new phase of living makes him again terribly vulnerable and anxious, and yet these circumstances have nothing necessarily to do with sin or evil in that person's life. Although this is relatively current thinking in the psychological world, it has been interesting to note that the Church realized the gravity of most of these same basic crises *over a thousand years ago* and set up sacramental means to help the believer face most of the same transitions within the loving and strengthening context of the body of believers.[8]

My own experience and investigation have led me to believe that committing my life as wholly as I can to God and receiving the reassuring sense of His Spirit does give me a deep and ultimate security my humanity has longed for. But, when and if one discovers that he is *again* anxious as a Christian, he can know that Christ counted on His disciples having troubled hearts and told them He was sending the Holy Spirit to comfort or

7. Erik H. Erikson's 'Eight Stages of Man', *Childhood and Society*, New York: Norton, 1950, pp. 219–233.

8. Note the similarity of Erikson's eight stages to the '*Seven Sacraments*' as historically recognized in the Church. See *The Book of Common Prayer* (1953 ed.), p. 607, for list.

'strengthen' them when they did (See John 14). So I have come to see that restlessness and ultimate dependency, like pain and evil, are woven into the fabric of life and that Christ does not abolish these for the Christian, but periodically they may become the motive power to drive us toward fulfilment in Him.[9]

Understanding this, however, has not changed the fact that I find it very unpleasant to be restless or discouraged. It is all very well to understand that God will teach me something from these inexplicable and anxious times and bring me closer to Himself, but they make me very lonely and it is quite another thing for me to find a practical way out of them. I have discovered that these periods often lead into long and unproductive sessions of introspection and discouragement.

9. I am here talking about periodic bouts with restlessness leading to anxiety about one's spiritual health. If, on the other hand, the Christian (or anyone else) finds that he is continually anxious or afraid, I would suggest that he go to a qualified counsellor. Many of our anxieties have physical and psychological roots and can be alleviated through counselling.

Chapter 7

OUT OF THE PIT OF INTROSPECTION—
A SLIPPERY BANK

'I will not leave you desolate ...'
John 14: 18 (RSV)

The only 'way out', I have found, of the sort of loneliness and despair that result from my long periods of self-centred introspection is this: a simple style of life I resist. I resist it because it seems too insignificant to change my condition, because it appears to be too much trouble and does not seem to involve important enough issues to fulfil my anxious needs for relatedness at such times. I also resist this way out because it might lead to rejection.

The process of discouragement in my life seems to work something like this: When I can't complete something on which I am working, when I become afraid about health or the future, or when things get sort of 'dry' or I get anxious—when these things start happening, I begin withdrawing into my soul and looking within in order to find out how to get back to happiness and be God's person. I start imagining disaster—everything from financial failure to my wife's infidelity or my children's possible unhappiness in life. But then, before I know it, I find that I am bogged down in self-pity and hopelessness, searching frantically for 'peace' and 'direction' and a way back to faith. As the situation gets to be insolvable, the search gets more and more urgent.

Again and again, I find that God brings me out of these pits by a simple yet seemingly impossible route. I finally get so sick of myself and of trying to see the blueprint for the next twenty years that I have to put down my spiritual binoculars and quit my frantic scanning of the horizons of my consciousness. Finally, alone and exhausted with my self-absorption, I may sit and cry and admit that I am lost, bogged down, and wrapped up in myself. I can truly see that 'there is no health in me'. As I confess my condition, I can often look back and realize that only in Him have I known hope in my own past. Then, at last, I give up. I give up my self-diagnosis and my frantic efforts to avoid failure, either physically, psychologically, or materially. And I give up my dreams for success. I give them to Him, finally being willing to have them fulfilled or not. And strangely, this is like dying, to give up these dreams of success in any venture, since my whole destiny seems to be riding on them. Then, since I have given up the 'big' plans for my life (being a psychologist, a writer, a success in business), I am interested only in sanity for today.[1] Paradoxically, it is at this point that I am ready to live again. Since I have ceased to worry about something unreal—the results of my life *tomorrow*, I am free to begin working with the building materials which are real—the hours in *today*. I begin slowly to wipe away the tears and blink in the morning light of a new day and to notice individuals immediately around me again. I begin to see the shapes

1. Or sometimes, if I am afraid of something, I have to stop and say to myself, 'Yes, this thing I fear *could* happen to me, but God would be there; and with Him as my audience I could start again to face the eventualities this event would bring about.' And sometimes this very *acceptance* of the possibility makes the spectre lose the sharpness of its horror.

of trees and flowers and the vastness of the sky, to hear the sounds of birds singing and quarrelling with each other, and children shouting and dogs barking—all of which have been going on 'out there' but which have been sealed off from the inner, windowless cell in which I do my serious worrying about myself.

It is impossible to describe what then takes place, except that it is at this point somewhere that healing begins for me. And strangely, I have to take the step of beginning again as an act of faith, since I do not *feel* like acting at all. It's just that I finally get so sick of going over and over my own situation until I could scream 'There is no solution for me!' . . . that I turn back to God. And when I can get beyond my compulsive desire to 'solve it all myself', I may be able to emerge from my cell. To walk out of it is a real act of faith since I get the feeling at such times that I *must* attend to the outcome of my problems or they will never get solved. But the truth seems to be that I am like my little girl who was continually picking the scab off a wound to see if it had healed. There is a sense in which I reach a point at which I have looked at my situation until any more direct attention to it, even in prayer, becomes a step away from Christ. I have to walk away in raw faith believing that God will work beneath the scab.

About this time in the process, some morning I wake up and *see* my wife again. I begin to concentrate on what is going on *with her*. I start forcing myself to listen carefully to the children at breakfast again. I start to ask questions to find out if I really know what they are saying and to let them know that I understand, when I do.

As I start out to work on such mornings, I begin to see

people as individuals again, persons with homes and families and needs. In short, I begin to live 'in the now', as described in the last chapter. At such times I often feel dead to happiness and optimism. Sometimes I am only keeping on for another hour—knowing numbly that this process of keeping on for Christ is the thread of faith which must lead to His will. And since no other process seems to help, I find myself at such times 'keeping on keeping on', partly out of obedience to Christ and partly out of a deep intuitive knowledge that painful and paradoxical as it is, personal suffering is a real and important part of the human way Jesus came to show us. J. B. Phillips was a real help to me in commenting that today we seem to 'assume that we have a "right" to be happy, a "right" to live without pain, and somehow, a "right" to be shielded from the ills which flesh is heir to. Evidently the early Christians thought no such thing. They quite plainly took it as an honour to suffer for Christ's sake, and here (in the New Testament) the advice is to accept all kinds of troubles, whether they are apparently for Christ's sake or not, as friends instead of resenting them as intruders.'[2]

As I have begun in these moments to try to crawl out of the slough of self toward Christ and others, I have realized that at least I can use my miserable days for Him by trying to love His people and do His will. Also, I have found that there is a strange dilation of the soul's eyes in 'keeping on' through one's suffering for Christ's sake. My own misery often makes me sensitive to the signs of lonely agony in other lives which I would have missed otherwise. Besides these things John Coburn speaks of the positive acceptance of one's own suffer-

2. J. B. Phillips, *Op. Cit.*, p. 70.

ing as a way of participating in a very real power
God releases into the world, a power which allows other
men to be strengthened to embrace and carry their own
burdens as they see us carrying ours.[3] This trying to do
God's will, this increased sensitivity to others, and this
possible release of power into the world—these things
at least give periods of anguish some meaning. And
through all this I have discovered what Frankl meant
when he said that 'suffering ceases to be suffering in
some way the moment it finds a meaning'.[4]

As I have forced myself to begin again in faith to live
once more in little ways, often before I know it, I have
felt the faint stirring of a fresh breeze through a life
which a day before had been stifled by self-pity and
oppressive loneliness. What I find happening on those
days when I begin to reach out to people around me in
personal ways—oh, such little ways—honestly listening,
really watching, is that I may become for that day a truly
Christ-like person, a caring man. And since I have then
started filling my thoughts and prayers with real people
and events instead of spectres and imagined disasters, my
prayers and Scripture reading deal less with the hypothetical and more with real life. And whatever may happen to my future, I have the feeling at the end of such
days of having lived as an authentic human being, reach-
ing out toward others as Christ did. At such times I have
understood how close Camus came unconsciously to
describing true Christian living when he made his hero

3. John B. Coburn, *Prayer and Personal Religion*, Philadel-
phia: Westminster Press, 1957, See Chapter on Suffering and Joy,
p. 90ff.
4. Viktor Frankl, *Man's Search for Meaning*, New York:
Beacon Press, 1964, p. 179.

say thoughtfully, 'Heroism and sanctity don't really ap-
peal to me, I imagine. What interests me is being a man',[5]
because the longer I am on this crazy Christian pilgrimage the less I want a static condition called 'saint-
hood'—or rather the more I believe that to *be* a saint is
simply to be a man, in the ordinary world, but to be
Christ's man. It seems more and more apparent to me
that to be a living child of God is to be a working ap-
prentice to a fantastically careful Artist in the field of
creating and sustaining life, freedom, and relatedness out
of the clay pits of loneliness and despair all around us,
this day.

It is impossible to overstate what this simple change of
focus has meant to me in terms of social contacts and
relationships in my daily living. In the competitive milieu
in which I have been brought up, I have only had time
for people who 'count', people whose destinies were
linked to mine in terms of social status or interests and
general economic desires. But I am finding in this new
perspective that people who might not have counted in
any of the old ways can be interesting and can be sub-
jects for my involved attention as *important* people in
themselves, because they are important to God.

These friendships are much more natural and deep because they are based on the sharing of the loneliness and
hopes which are the very foundation blocks of our common humanity. Such friendships do not have to be
pumped up by the compressed air of frenzied, score-
keeping social functions. And the great dawning insight
of this perspective to me is that if the ordinary, 'unimportant', people in the world become interesting and

5. Albert Camus, *The Plague*, New York: Alfred A. Knopf,
1948, p. 231.

fun to be with, and if even loneliness and discouragement
have value in learning to live for Christ—then *any place*,
any job or vocation or marriage can be a place of fulfilment and potential happiness. I saw in retrospect that for
so long it had been much too important to be with *the*
sharpest people in sight. When I wasn't with 'them', I felt
restless and not fulfilled somehow. But through the
changing of the focus of my attention, God is opening
the doorway to the world of His people; the people
along the paths I am walking today who fear, hate, suffer, and hope and who are waiting for Love to come and
fill their lives.

And what happens to me as I bring up from the almost dry well of my own life a few small cups of water
for people around me and begin to pay attention to them
and love them? I sometimes find, after a day, a week, a
month, that the anxiety and hollow dryness are gone.
While I have been looking the other way into people's
lives, I have again been made new by participating in
His love.

In thinking about the fact that Christian love brings
healing to its bearers as well as to those into whose life it
is focused, I began to wonder why I often found it so
difficult to love as a Christian.

Chapter 8

A NEW FREEDOM ABOUT LOVING

'*A new commandment I give to you, that you love one another . . .*'

John 13: 34 (RSV)

For some years I faced a question which bothered me in the growing company of changing lives. There was more talk of 'Christian love' than I was used to. Although I felt loved and accepted by many of these people in a way I never had before, I was uneasy about my own lack of selfless love (*agape*) for many of them. I did love *some* of them, but usually they were either the attractive ones or those who evidenced a real concern about me, and I knew that this was the same old exchange-mart love Erich Fromm and others described so well as characteristic of our capitalistic and consumer type living.[1] Yet, although I did not *feel* very loving much of the time, I had to admit that in my daily living I was helping people I had not even noticed before. And I was doing things as a Christian to reach out to people in situations I had always ignored. This was taking place sort of naturally as I began to see people from the new perspective into which I was moving. But there was seldom the warm selfless feeling I had always felt should be central to the experience of Christian love. I prayed about this, read about it, and asked about it. Although

1. Erich Fromm, *Op. Cit.*, p. 108ff.

some Christians confessed that they too did not really have much Christian love for the unlovely and it concerned them, this was little comfort to me.

One day as I was thinking about this question of the experience of Christian love, a scene flashed on to the screen of my imagination. I was sitting on our front porch and our youngest daughter was riding her tricycle down the driveway toward the street. I noticed that from up the street a huge removal van was coming very fast. The driver's brake had slipped, and he was coming faster and faster down the hill in front of our house. In a horrified moment I realized that my little girl was heading out into the street right in front of that truck, and that because of a hedge she could not see the truck coming! Without even thinking, I jumped across the porch rail and ran for the street, realizing at the last second that I could dive and push the tricycle beyond the wheels, but that I could never get out of the way myself. Then I was diving. Just as I pushed the tricycle beyond the truck, I felt and heard a horrible *crunch* as the huge wheel ran right across my back. Even though this scene took place only in my imagination, I was weak just thinking about it. Here was a real act of love, 'laying down one's life', and I hoped I would do that if the situation ever actually came up.

But as I sat there thinking about this, a nasty little boy from down the street came riding by in front of our house. He's the one who picks his nose all the time and who had laughed and made nasty signs at me when I had tried to catch him to talk to him about throwing stones at my little girl the day before. Although I like most children, I do not like this one. But as I watched him ride by, the same scene I had been through a few minutes before started replaying itself in my imagination. Only this time the nasty little boy was the one riding down our driveway toward the path of the hurtling truck. I hesitated, this wasn't my child. But then, although I did not even *like* the boy, I found myself jumping the rail and running for the street. Again I dived and pushed the tricycle beyond the truck's wheels. And again I was crushed.

In thinking about these two experiences, the haunting question came to my mind: *Which of these two was the greater act of Christian love? To save my own daughter or the child from down the street?* And the answer I could not get away from was *to die for the child down the street.* Any pagan would try to save his own daughter. And yet there was *no warm feeling of love at all* in the second loving act. I had not even *wanted* to help him. Now I began to get excited. If this were true, then perhaps Christian love is not what I had always thought it was. I went back to the New Testament to see what love looked like there in the light of this new experience.

Turning first to the 13th chapter of I Corinthians, I saw that love is the most important gift and will outlast all the others. To examine Christian love in action, I thought: *Where would I turn to see the greatest example of God's kind of love in action.* And of course I thought of Christ's giving of Himself. As I read the accounts of Christ's life, I saw something I had never seen before. I was re-reading the Gospel reports of the last hours before the Crucifixion. Here was the One who had come to Jerusalem, no doubt aware of the personal danger this trip involved. He had looked at Jerusalem and wept. Now He was coming towards some sort of climax in His

sense of mission. Then there follows that strange scene in
Gethsemane (Matthew 26; Luke 22). Jesus leaves even
His most trusted friends and goes off a little way by
Himself to pray about continuing in the direction His
life and ministry seemed to be taking. As I read, I
thought: *Now here is real love in action. Here Jesus is
approaching the act which changed the world's concep-
tion of what love in human form is like. Why can't I feel
that way about loving men?* But as I read on I was
shocked. I read the account again. But what I thought I
had seen was true. Jesus was evidently *not* filled with a
warm *feeling* of loving desire to die for man. As a matter
of fact, our term for extreme discomfort, 'sweating
blood', probably came from His experience that night.
He evidently 'sweated blood' and prayed three times for
a way *not* to perform this most loving act. And when He
did agree to do it, the love was expressed not by His *feeling* but by the fact that He acted out of love for His
father *whether He felt like it or not!*[2]

If this is true, then Christian love is not based on the
feeling I had always longed for. Christian love is simply
an act of the kind God wants performed for another
person's health and wholeness to help fulfil His will for
that person. And my *performing* that act in Christ's

2. I am aware of the current controversy over the source of
several of these verses and that my use of this scene bypasses the
whole question of what Jesus in his humanity actually knew in
the garden about the ultimate value of the next day's actions. But
my point is that whatever He knew, He apparently based His decision in facing the crisis of risking His life not on a warm feeling
about the results of the action nor its benefits to others, but on
His loving obedience to His Father's will as He could determine
it. For a brief but excellent scholarly treatment of the human-
divine question regarding Jesus see *The Humanity and Divinity
of Christ* by John Knox, Cambridge University Press, 1967.

perspective and concern is the *love*, not my warm feeling *about* doing it. Then I began to see that all through the Scriptures and the Church's history the greatest acts of love were often accompanied by circumstances which must have been very unpleasant and distasteful for the Christian. I realized that I had always interpreted the joyful obedience to *God* which these acts demonstrated as a 'warm feeling' *about the unpleasant act*. Evidently, I had assumed that Paul's beatings and the fires of martyrdom or the nails of the cross didn't really hurt because of the warm Hollywood-type feeling of love. Further, I had noticed before that Christ *commanded* His disciples to love each other (John 13: 34, 35). I saw why that command had disturbed me in the past. No one can command *his feelings* for others. But one *can* command to a far greater degree his concerned *actions* towards others.

So now I realised that from Christ's perspective I was not to pray for a feeling of love for my fellow man, but rather for the courage to act in love toward him in specific situations, whatever my spiritual temperature read at the time, or whether or not I felt loving that day. And the strangest thing began to happen. Occasionally the feeling I had longed for about people has come along after the act of love or concern had passed or in the midst of it. It then became clear that this feeling is a gift that may or may not accompany the act of love.

But there is a problem here. If one is loving others out of 'obedience', people have told me, the 'good turns' are cold and impersonal and cause resentment on the part of the party being loved. But I am not talking about *that* kind of attitude. The kind of specific love I am referring to is paradoxical, in that, although I may be motivated to reach out to others *because* of Christ, I still find myself doing the loving thing *for* the person. In other words, from the recipient's perspective you are not acting toward him impersonally, out of duty to a remote God, but the person *feels loved* as you move toward him into his life's sphere. This paradoxical truth keeps this kind of love from being a legalistic obligation . . . which would certainly be recognized as such by the recipient.

In any case, I have given up beating myself with a chain when I do not feel love. I am free to begin finding natural ways to bring the kind of love and concern to people which I would want to bring if I felt the warm feeling.[3] I believe now that my greatest days of loving from Christ's perspective may be those days on which I don't even feel well, much less loving. And yet I reach out toward another person in his perhaps hostile frenzy, simply because this is Christ's way and I feel that He would want me to do the simple act with which I am confronted. Of course, there is emotional feeling involved in such acts, but not the kind I had looked for.

It was finally getting through to me that active Christian love does not look the same from the vantage point of the lover, as it does from the perspective of the on-

3. It is interesting to note that many psychologists following Guthrie and others are beginning to believe that contrary to common belief, feelings *follow* behaviour change instead of preceding it. (For instance an alcoholic, perhaps out of sheer desperation, forces himself to go to an AA meeting, not feeling like it at all. But once he has taken the step and *changed his behaviour* to the extent of going, he may come to have *feelings* of hope for a new life—instead of a wonderful, hopeful feeling coming *first*, *convincing* him to give up drinking.) Whereas, for years we Christians have tried to get our attitudes right *first*. I am saying that my experience has been that if I begin *acting* in love, often the feeling of love may follow.

looker. At about that time, I remember talking to Gertrude Behanna.[4] We were discussing the problems we were finding in trying to communicate the reality of Christ. Since I think she is one of the most gifted communicators in the Church, I was particularly interested in one comment she made. She said that she had just returned from speaking to several hundred people at a large meeting. She had not felt well before she got up to speak, and as she went through her piece' she did not feel very effective nor very loving. She told me that she was just doing what she had come to do for her Lord—to deal with the problems she sensed the people faced and tell them about Christ and His message. For Gert it was a rather matter of fact presentation as far as her feelings were concerned, and she is a person of great emotional power. But afterwards, she was amazed to note that person after person came up and said, 'I have never experienced Jesus Christ so clearly in an individual's life as I did in yours tonight.' She told me that she felt embarrassed, almost like a fraud for not telling them that she was *not* feeling at all Christlike. As we talked, I remembered similar experiences in the lives of other Christian leaders. And I believe that what had happened was that Gert's willing involvement with the people and their problems (*even when she did not feel particularly Christian or even feel like being there*) put her unconsciously very much in the perspective of her Lord on the cross; and the people saw this incarnate in the selfgiving of her life. She was not being religious, she was being Gert in obedience to her Father, and this did not *feel* loving at all *to her*. If someone had asked her that night how Christian love feels

4. Author of *The Late Liz*, New York: Appleton-Century, 1957.

from the viewpoint of the loving one, her answer might
have been simply, 'tired'.

And such loving acts can be very powerful if they are
specific. But I do not think this notion is generally shared
in Christian groups. People often ask the question, 'How
can I be more loving?' But that is a meaningless question
in the abstract. It is like asking a golfer which club to
use. It has no meaning apart from a specific set of circumstances. So I began to get very interested in trying to
see the nature of individual acts of love when I could
spot them. And the results of this kind of obedience continue to amaze me in terms of the significant events
which often follow seemingly unimportant but specific
acts of love.

Several years ago I attended a weekend conference at
which a very close friend of mine, a businessman, was
one of the conference leaders. We had talked about
Christian love a lot that weekend. At one of the final
sessions, this friend, whom I shall call Dick, told the
people at the conference the following story: When he
was a small boy, his father, a restless man who drank
quite a bit, had left his mother and had married a much
younger woman. Although his mother had remarried
and Dick had a stepfather whom he came to love and
respect, he had always deeply resented his real father for
leaving the family. Over the years they had met only a
few times—often leaving additional scars, as Dick's dad
would promise to give him presents and then forget to
send them, adding disappointment and weight to the
rejection he had known. Then, as an adult, my friend had
met a man who really believed in God. Through this
man's presentation of the Christian message, Dick tried
to give God a life he felt was shaky and insecure on the

inside, though outwardly very successful, and Dick had become an outstanding Christian layman. Then almost ten years later, he had been asked to speak at this weekend Christian conference. As he was preparing to come to the conference, Dick got word that his real father was dying with cancer of the throat in a city near the conference centre. He did not want to see him at all. He simply had nothing to say to him. The cancer had advanced until his father could not talk or hear and was going blind. His only communication with the world outside his mind was through the process of writing and reading on one of those little toy magic slates, which he could barely see.

One of Dick's Christian friends had gone to see the father and told him on the magic slate that his son had grown into a fine man. He asked the older man if he knew that Dick had become a Christian. The father, who was not a Christian, shook his head. He then wrote on the slate that more than just about anything he would love to see his son. He said that although he had never been much of a father, he had been very proud of his boy. He was sorry that he had hurt his mother and him. The friend left the hospital and wrote to Dick. Although Dick did not want to see his dad, since he was coming that way anyway, he decided to go by the hospital before the conference to see him. When Dick got there he went into the room alone and faced his father. They just looked at each other for several minutes; then Dick began to write on the slate. He told his dad that he loved him and about how his own life had changed since they had last been together because he had tried to give his future to God. His dad did not really understand but was glad and wanted to hear more about what had happened. As the minutes moved on in silence, one man wrote and then, after changing the slate, the other. Dick gently told his dying father about the Lord who had saved him from so much of the misery that his father had known. Afterwards they just sat and looked at each other. Finally Dick got up to leave. Then, with all his experience of the rejections of a lifetime telling him not to do it, he turned back and picked up the slate, 'Dad,' he wrote, 'would you like to give your life to Christ too?' His dad stared at the slate for a long time in silence, frowning. Then he took the stylus and wrote, 'Yes, I would. But I don't know how. Will you show me, Dick?' And with tears welling up in his eyes, Dick led his own father to a new beginning as he gave as much of himself as he could to as much of Christ as he could accept. Then they prayed together for the first and only time in their lives—on a magic slate.

As Dick was telling the conference participants about this experience, he asked them to pray with him for his father and his father's wife and family—that they would not be afraid. That weekend at the conference three men and their wives, who lived in the city nearby where the hospital was, made newer and deeper turnings of their lives to God. They decided they wanted to try to begin expressing God's love in some specific little ways. When they got back home, one of them called every hospital in the city until he found Dick's dad. And although this man hated to visit hospitals—as a matter of fact had always refused to do so before, they went to visit Dick's father and told him they had just become Christians too. The wives helped his family, who knew almost no-one in the city. Although Dick's dad went blind shortly after that time and lost all verbal contact with the world, the new Christians kept coming until he died. They sat and held his hand so that he would not be afraid. These Christian friends then quietly made the funeral arrangements and later helped the widow get a job. The day of the funeral a friend of Dick's was talking to the attractive widow after the service. She was very tired. She said in a thoughtful but uncomprehending way, 'I've never seen people like that,' nodding towards Dick's friends. 'We didn't even know them. I would give anything to have what they have found.' And standing there in the car park after the funeral the woman heard for the first time that she could make a new beginning and accept the love of God which she had run from all her life—until she saw it incarnate in a few ordinary men and women who stopped by a hospital room to tentatively try a tiny act of love.

Chapter 9

RESPONSIBLE LOVING RELATIONSHIPS BETWEEN MEN AND WOMEN

'. . . you must no longer live as the Gentiles do . . .'
Ephesians 4: 17 (RSV)

About the same time that I was beginning to realize the power of loving people specifically, I found myself confronted with a growing number of counselling situations concerning the sexual aspects of love. People seemed to have no Christian orientation to deal with loving relationships between committed Christian men and women.

I suppose I had assumed that because secular books and magazines for the past fifteen years have been discussing in great detail the problems of men and women in working out sexual adjustments within and outside of marriage, Christians, who had decided they wanted to commit their lives to Christ, had faced these questions together and come up with some teaching guidelines. For a long time, as a new Christian, I was able to ignore such questions, at least I tried to ignore them, but when I began to try consciously to become aware of God's presence with me in every area of my life, it was not long before I had to face the question as a Christian man and husband: 'What about the sexual part of life?' At first I unconsciously 'excused myself' from God when either thinking about or engaging in anything which might be considered overtly sexual. But I realized this behaviour implied that there was something basically unwholesome about sex. And since sex is evidently a universal God-given drive, I was confused about my tending implicitly to seal off this area of my inner experience from the creative presence of Christ. In reading the Scriptures I had concluded that sex is a good thing, a gift from God to help us overcome our loneliness (Genesis 2:18) and to signify and complete the inner spiritual joining of a man and woman in marriage. I felt that sexual union was a sacramental means of expressing the yearning of two people to join their personal inner lives into one. But when I tried to find out how other Christians faced the troublesome problems inherent in *living* as a sexual being, I ran into a strange blank wall. So I began to re-examine some of the questions which came from Christian young people, ministers, and business men who were struggling to live and communicate their faith in the midst of great moral change all around them.

'Is the Christian concept of fidelity in marriage outdated?'

If sexual union is God's gift to signify and complete the spiritual or emotional joining of a man and woman, then why the Christian insistence on only one partner? [1] If we are supposed to love all people, then why not seal this love *in as many cases as possible* with the outward sign of physical union? To a good many young people in the Church today the rule of not going outside the marriage relationship sexually is an antiquated sociological hangover from another kind of culture and family

1. The standard answer is: because God was pretty clear about this in the 7th Commandment (Exodus 20:14). And that's really good enough for me. But I find it encouraging when these basic commandments make sense on other grounds too.

structure. But even from a humanist perspective the Hebrews had unusual insight into the human situation, and it occurred to me that the fact that their earliest recorded code of law (Exodus 20: 1–17) expressly forbids adultery might have some deep psychological basis, besides meeting the more obvious needs of a nomadic culture. Such a commandment would not be a part of the 'all time top ten' unless it was pretty significantly tied to the foundations of the human situation. As I began checking through the basic documents of the faith, I was struck by statements like that of the author of Proverbs who said that a man who commits adultery does not have good sense, that in fact he is destroying his very soul (Proverbs 6: 32). So I began to think through my own life to see if this had any existential meaning to me as a modern man.

If the sexual joining of a man and wife is an outward expression of an inner reality—the joining of two whole lives—then it seems to me that a lot more is involved in the act of sexual intercourse than a physical meeting. I think sexual union has to do with woman's strange need to be mother, wife, lover, sharer of pain with man, and builder of a nest to receive and complete a man's strength and creative virility.[2]

In our marriage we have found that the uniqueness of monogamous sexual union has to do with our need for a special place or emotional home in the world. There seems to be a great fulfilment for a woman in helping her man when he comes home to take off the armour of sophistication in which he must do battle in the world,

2. I am not saying that all of these yearnings are instinctive. Most of them, when experienced, are probably sociologically conditioned. But I think these desires have grown out of the context of the Judeo-Christian tradition, which I believe is based on the best information we have about man's deepest needs.

competitively playing the game of business or profession to provide for her and her brood. But if her man knows she is intimate sexually with another man, then psychologically how can he really let the bars down and come home to rest his spiritual head in her lap? How can he take off his emotional armour and have his strength completed? For he is too vulnerable; he is still in competition, being compared with others, as he is everywhere else in the world. How can he in his insecurity just be himself? And if a woman knows her husband is with other women, her sacrifice of all other men for him is somehow spoiled. She may *not* be the source of his human physical renewal. How can she be a loving open child, freely sharing her most intimate secret? For she, too, is being compared and used as one among others. Just as the Bible tells us that God is a jealous God about our unique commitment to Him among other objects of worship (Exodus 20: 5), we, who are made in His image, are jealous of those who threaten to replace our uniqueness with our wives or husbands. This jealousy can be deeply painful whether or not anything even remotely concerning the sex act is involved. The one-partner plan of Christian marriage provides great psychological security in making allowance for the ebb and flow of life from public to private. Also, the deep seated need for ultimate relatedness, which makes us seek God, can find a partial expression in the sacrament of marriage.[3]

3. If you find you are continually jealous, I would recommend that you seek help from a marriage counsellor or professional therapist. Much jealousy in marriage is unwarranted by the facts and may indicate some deeper personal insecurities in the life of the jealous party, just as much philandering may be a sign of deep insecurity on the part of the Don Juan.

Another reason for limiting one's self to a single sexual partner in marriage seems to me to be an extremely practical one. If I am honest, sexual needs have tended to drive me toward reconciliation when we have been separated through disagreements. And the paradoxical thing is that the physical act of coming together, because of past associations of love, sometimes creates an atmosphere in which our perspectives change and we can again love each other emotionally and spiritually.

'What about the dangers of sexual intimacy in the openness of life together in small groups?'

But what happens to us in the Christian community, in the body of Christ? If sexual expression is a God-given gift of grace for the overcoming of physical and emotional loneliness between man and woman, it is inextricably bound into the Gospel. For the Gospel is also concerned with the overcoming of the separation of people, as well as the separation between man and God. The sense of aloneness and incompleteness even in 'Christian' marriages is so well known that to mention it is to describe it for many people.[4] So when a person is converted and decides to commit his whole future to the living Christ, he begins to feel the release from the awful threat of a lonely and meaningless future. He meets other radiant, changing Christians in small groups. Together, they begin to find freedom and acceptance, just

4. Although this is not the place to discuss the tragic sexual drifting apart which so often takes place in Christian marriages after a few years because of breakdowns in communication, I think we must learn to face together aş couples our inability even to talk about our deepest needs in this area. Reuel Howe has done an excellent job of discussing this delicate subject in *The Creative Years*, New York: Seabury Press, 1965.

as they are, and a place to be personal about the simple aches and joys of life one experiences in trying to live for Christ—which many of them cannot discuss in their marriages. People become open and really love each other. Although nothing may be said about sex, this can be a very sexual situation, in the broader sense of which I have been speaking. The kind of openness and accept-ance among Christians is that which everyone longs for in marrage, and which in marriage would naturally lead to a complete giving of ourselves to each other. But Christ is the centre of Christian groups, and the know-ledge that He has saved us from despair and from our-selves helps us to appreciate as brothers and sisters this wonderful gift of spiritual closeness. Because of a com-mon commitment to Christ and the finding of His will, this acceptance of each other is usually just a wonderful and creative experience.

As I began to accept the love of God and find the freedom to open my life to other people, particularly to Christians in a small group, I began to see that in the loving Christian fellowship we are dealing with some very powerful and basic human needs. Most of us in our generation are so starved for any kind of love and true acceptance that when we open our lives to God and to our fellow Christians, we may find ourselves at some time thinking of the bedroom instead of the upper room. And this can be a real surprise when you think your motives are purely spiritual.

I intended not even to mention this, because I do not feel that this is a general problem in trying to see life from Christ's perspective. But as I have been sitting here deciding, I have seen, against the white wall across my office, the haunted faces of several of my Christian friends, who have found themselves inexplicably trapped in tragic situations. I remember especially listening to one lovely Christian woman. Through tears and stunned with amazement, almost disbelief; she told me that she had committed adultery, although she had never thought it even a possibility for her. And during these past few years I have spent hours talking to men and women, ministers and laymen, who are deeply committed to Christ but who in one way or the other have told me the same story.

What does an active lay person do to avoid this sort of problem? In talking this matter over with some very perceptive Christians, I have come to believe that a deep understanding of the weakness of the human will is a good start. But in talking to lay people about counselling as Christians, I have found a couple of practical suggestion helpful with regard to relationships between men and women:

(1) Any time a man or woman sets up a *continuing* relationship with a member of the opposite sex in an *un*structured situation in which they are together privately, the chances of some kind of sexual involvement *not* taking place would appear to be small. And the fact that the content of the discussion is 'Christianity' or 'prayer', seems to make almost no difference. . . . As a matter of fact, there may be a broader truth in the old cliché 'couples who pray together, stay together', than is generally recognized.

(2) For non-professional counselling over a period of time, I have found it better for men to counsel with men and women with women. A Christian lay Sunday School teacher or small group leader who finds himself doing a

lot of counselling can usually scout around and find a perceptive Christian woman to whom he can refer women who want to have someone with whom to pray and discuss personal problems regarding their faith over a period of time.

(3) Since a lot of the new lay counselling goes on at conferences in resort type settings, I have found that it is not a good thing for me to counsel with women privately in my hotel room (or theirs) late at night. This may seem over cautious, but this type of intimate meeting alone to talk about loneliness and problems in marriage can be a considerable strain on non-present spouses, not to mention the danger of latent gamesmanship.

I know many of you may think I am either over pious or a lecherous ogre for taking the time to deal with such a seemingly outlandish problem. But because of my own experience, the tragedies in the lives of some strong and dedicated Christian friends, and the unfortunate degeneration of some small group experiments of the past, I am taking the risk of discussing these problems. I know that the tendency on the part of some Christians is to say, 'Well, if there is a chance for anything like *that* happening, let's not get mixed up in small groups.' But that would be a tragic attitude to take. In the first place the strength and companionship of a Christian fellowship have *kept many people from* the desperation of trading their bodies for some personal love and attention. Besides, any time there is real life and healing going on, there are dangers of excesses. Look at any of the reformations of the past. One of my friends, whom I respect tremendously, suggested that I delete this section, because 'people are just looking for a way to discredit lay renewal.' But I think the time has come to face openly both the problems and the joys of the Christian life. At least, those who commit themselves to Christ now will not be with a bunch of people who are afraid to face the dangers as well as the opportunities of real living. I personally believe our generation is looking for this open attitude instead of that which has so often prevailed in the church of, 'Oh, we must not talk about that or they will think . . .' If anyone thinks these sorts of problems are new in the Christian community, check Paul's letters to the earliest small Christian groups (e.g. I Corinthians 5: 1).

'How does a deeply committed Christian face the problem of sexual lust?'

Ever since I was a young boy in high school I have liked girls. This disposition has brought a good bit of conflict as well as happiness into my experience. When I became a Christian, Mary Allen and I loved each other and had a marriage which seemed very good to us, a marriage which we were both trying to make better. I wasn't committing adultery, and we were very much in love, so I thought this was one area in which I would not have immediate problems as a Christian. But in discussions, by the silence I encountered, I began to get the idea that for many Christians sex is an evil area of life. Because of this, I began to be more conscious of committing those casual, fleeting 'walking down the street' adulteries in my imagination. These little scenarios were so natural I had not even thought of them as adulteries until I read that Christ said that every man who looks at a woman lustfully has already committed adultery with her in his heart (Matthew 5:28).[5] That statement, if true, gave adultery a real home in my inner life.

At first I was horrified. I said to myself, 'Man, if giving up noticing good looking women is a prerequisite for getting into heaven, I know three things: (1) I'll never make it, (2) There's no need for me to witness to my friends because they would never make it either, and (3) What kind of men will there be in Heaven with whom I would *want* to spend an eternity?'

But as I began to look more closely at the dynamics of this almost universal experience of noticing, as a reflex action, the potential sexual compatibility of a member of the opposite sex, I began to realize what I had done. I had identified the instant (and automatic) *recognition* I have just described with the *subsequent imaginary episode of committing adultery* with the person noticed.

5. In the context in which this passage is set, I think Jesus was trying to tell his listeners that purity from God's perspective was something they could not even understand in terms of their legalistic viewpoint. The kind of goodness which is demanded by God in terms of perfection *none* of them had. And Christ began to cut the ground from under their pitiful legalistic type of righteousness. He told them their goodness would have to be far greater than that of the scribes and Pharisees before they could set foot in the kingdom of Heaven. For instance, He continued, 'You have heard that it was said . . .' (and He named 'outer' sins) 'but,' He continued, 'I say to you . . .' and He went on to tell them that true purity involves the *inner* as well as the *outer* expression of the desires, and He listed inner adultery, etc. and caught them all.

Fortunately, with this delineation of Godly perfection comes the news that we are saved by grace through faith (Ephesians 2:8). But I think Christians should be perfectly clear that historically Christianity has taken a definite stand against adultery and filling one's imagination with fantasies of adultery. It is amazing what regular church attendance and a pious mask can cover up in a deacon's or sidesman's . . . or a minister's inner life (or that of their wives).

I have found that becoming a deeply committed Christian does not keep one from being fully aware of beauty in the opposite sex. And I do not think this *recognition* is in any sense sin nor is it an indication that one needs a spiritual check-up. In fact, if you do *not* recognize physical beauty in the opposite sex, and you are my age, *you* may need a *physical* check-up. And I am very serious. 'Recognition' in my opinion is never sin. As a matter of fact, recognition of specific possibility for sinning is a *prerequisite* for the development of Christian character. For instance, a blind man would not be considered honest for not stealing gold on a table before him —only a man who saw the gold and *recognized* fully his drive for it but chose not to steal it. Besides if temptation is sin, then Christ was *not* sinless, for He was tempted (see Luke 4: 1–13). It is what one *does* with that which is recognized that causes the problems.

Over six hundred years ago, Thomas 'A. Kempis discussed the process of succumbing to temptation with great clarity. He described a coming into the mind of an evil thought, followed by a strong elaborating of the thought as it is led by the thinker into the inner chamber of the imagination; 'then a sense of delight; then a perverse impulse and assenting'.[6] He points out that the only practical place to stop temptation is at the point of seeing or recognizing, 'for the enemy is more easily overcome if he is refused entrance to the door of the mind, and resisted on the threshold at the first knock'.[7] After the first assenting and turning the situation over to the imagination, the outcome seems to be pretty well de-

6. Thomas 'A Kempis, *The Imitation of Christ*, London: William Collins and Sons Co., Ltd., 1957, p. 50.
   7. *Ibid.*

cided. So the only place one may be able to stop the process is at the point of recognition.

I realize that all this may seem strange material to be included in a book about trying to see life from a new perspective as a Christian. But I have listened to some apparently sophisticated Christian people who are guilt-ridden inside over these and other very common personal issues. And having wondered alone about so many things, I am just getting a few out in the open so that you can consider them. Because of the constant exposure to sexually attractive people on T.V., in magazines, and on the street, there is no way to hide as a Christian, even if one chose to. But if you really become concerned with the amount of your attention which is absorbed by lust, you can change the activity in your imagination to an amazing degree by varying your selection of books, magazines, and films. As Martin Luther put it a good many years ago. 'You cannot keep the birds from flying over your head, but you can keep them from nesting in your hair.'

Part 3

A PERSONAL PERSPECTIVE

FOCUSED ON LIFE IN

THE INSTITUTIONAL CHURCH

Chapter 10

MEANWHILE, BACK AT THE CHURCH—FRUSTRATION

'. . . But God has so adjusted the body . . . that there may be no discord . . .'
                                    I Corinthians 12: 24, 25 (RSV)

Having seen that life with Christ can be real and that a Christian can face the present and begin to learn to love other people personally and responsibly, I began to hope that this might become the experience of the modern Church. I started to examine my life in the institutional setting of the Church. I had put this off for years and pretended that everything was 'all right' about the Church. I would say things like: 'There are just different ways of being God's people', and of course there *are*. But in my case this statement was a dishonest evasion of the problem of facing my own relationship with that branch of the Church to which my family and I belong. I realized that for many years I had been inwardly sick of the Church's programmes. But I had also supported these programmes by my gifts, my vote, and by my presence when required. Many times as a layman and as a business man I have wanted to shout out in committee meetings, 'Men, we are not doing anything which is relevant to anyone's *real* needs—*even our own*. We are just keeping the church machine going because . . . well,

because we don't know anything else to do! For God's
sake, let's take a new look at what we are doing!'

But I never did shout it because officers of the Church
are community leaders, men of responsibility; and they
and I—and the minister—all sitting there so seriously,
seemed to represent a sort of implicit unquestionable-
ness about the fact that things *must* go on that way. Besides being personally afraid of their rejection of me as
some sort of a young religious fanatic, I also had to
admit to myself that I honestly could not think of any
realistically constructive way to change the operation.
Further, speaking out against the Church's basic stance
in America at that time was rather like speaking against
motherhood. So to assuage my cowardice and frustration, I voiced my opinions strongly on specific issues
which cluttered our meetings—like whether we should
have a coke machine in the parish hall or put basketball
goals on the parking area. I now believe we spent so
much time on such issues because we were a *lot* more
clear about our economic policies than our theological
ones. I was always glad when my time to serve on committees was over. But in retrospect I found that in some
cases everyone, including the minister, felt the same
sense of frustration with the nature of the life we lived
together in those meetings.

As a result of my first conscious attempt as an adult
to make a commitment of my *life* to the living God, I
began to understand that God accepted me with all of
my shortcomings, some of which I was now becoming
secure enough to see. I became so excited about the new
life I was finding that I had to speak out in Church and
committee meetings. I knew that the meaning and purpose I had longed for were real and must be available to

other people because *I was finding them.* Somehow *the Church's programme* should provide a way that this could happen to others who had become discouraged with life. It was only when I began to suggest changing the Church's programme that I found out about conflict as a Christian. Because when I spoke out, my ideas and enthusiasm were met with a sort of embarrassed silence. Suggestions I made were either subtly tabled, or I was made 'chairman of a committee to investigate'. When I did investigate and offered suggestions, I found that I was somehow on a different wavelength from most of the Church officers I knew. People simply did not see what I was now seeing. I could not blame them since I had spent years in the Church and not seen that God could 'come alive' to people like me and change the whole meaning of being a Christian. Since I did not know what to do in terms of a new programme, I was very frustrated in church meetings. The minister we had at that time was a fine man, but he had tried programmes for years. And with all his efforts and integrity he had found no way to motivate people to get involved in these programmes at more than a token level. He was tired. And now he was somehow playing the game with us, dutifully reminding us of our 'spiritual obligations'—but basically, it seemed to me, thinking in terms of corporate business methods and results, though he did not know this, since he had never been in a corporate business structure. But I began to realize that the problem was not primarily a disagreement about methods, as it seemed to be on the surface. Rather we had a much deeper difference—in our basic perspectives. We no longer meant the same things when we spoke of 'the Christian life'.

As I saw more clearly the sickness and self-centred-

ness in my own life, I also began to see the sickness and
self-centredness in our corporate church life. The difference was that, personally, I was becoming free to confess
my phoney ways, when I could see them, and find
acceptance and forgiveness. This was freeing me to take
risks and, for the first time, to think creatively about
relationships and purpose in church programmes. Consequently, I began to shake off activities which, for me,
were unreal. I saw that *life did not have to be the way it
always had been*. My life was becoming an adventure. I
became interested in people's needs and actually cared
about some of them. But in the organizational life of the
Church, no one seemed to see that there was even anything wrong, much less that a *whole new experience of
living was waiting just outside our humdrum life together*.

I made awful mistakes and unconsciously intimidated
people by my implicit rejection of their faith and practice, as I tried to express mine. We were in several
churches in different cities during that time. I taught in
Sunday School and began to try to communicate personally that which I was finding. But the more people
began to believe what I was saying, the more trouble the
Church had. People whispered about 'cliques' and 'dangers'. I began to see the terrible threat that the kind of
meaning of the Gospel I was finding can pose to those
who are not finding a 'new experience of life'. Because,
from the outside this 'new' life looks like an emotional
and socially naïve 19th century piety, which it is not. I
also saw how threatened *I* was at the Church's rejection
of that which was becoming increasingly real to me. I
remember a prominent theological professor asking in
effect 'Who do you people think you are to criticize the

Church when it has had two thousand years of corporate universal experience to its credit.' And I felt a little subdued. Who were we indeed? But I simply *could not deny what was happening in my life* and in the lives of those whom I now knew in many denominations. Their experience was so much like mine that I felt as if we were in the same family. And the spirit we were finding had the aroma of the New Testament Church about it. And the fruits were love and peace and creative purpose towards others. For the first time I could speak about the Christian life with authority, because I knew that life inside my own skin was different. But I began to feel that I was fighting a hopeless battle in trying to express this faith in my own church. And I could not for the life of me figure out why.

Gradually, the real focus of my Christian life moved away from the institutional programme of the denomination to which we belonged. I found small but growing interdenominational groups whose purpose and witness clearly seemed to be to lead men and women into the new style of life I was finding. In the joy and acceptance of this exciting and open fellowship there was not time to worry about the problems of the institutional Church. We were communicating with amazing ease in these small groups, and many of us were experiencing a real love for other human beings. Genuine transformations were taking place in behaviour, attitudes, and relationships. People were being freed from alcoholism, families were being healed, and compulsives were finding peace. People flocked together in larger and larger local, regional, and even national meetings to share the insights, love, and adventure we were finding in our own small groups.

But the lay renewal movement was growing so fast that its energies had to be spent almost entirely on helping large numbers of new people to start learning the disciplines involved in living the Christian life. Those of us who were deeply involved emotionally or professionally in this movement found ourselves swamped with speaking engagements and with developing conference programmes and techniques having to do largely with helping people to *begin* the 'committed Christian life'. Later we started helping those who had begun trying to live for God themselves, to learn to help others begin. We made terrible mistakes and oversimplified many things. We had looked at the institutions' programmes and found them mostly to be academically orientated and not psychologically practical in the threatening world of the layman.

After a few exhausting but exhilarating years, I stepped back and tried to see what had happened. It seemed to me that in one sense the 'God is alive' Christians of America were divided roughly into two groups. On the one hand, there was a great and continually multiplying body of new or 'renewed' Christians trying openly to commit their whole lives to God. This group's success numerically in getting lay people to *begin* a new life was in danger of causing us to produce a generation of highly motivated witnessing Christians who would only know how to live the *first year* of the Christian life.[1]

1. This last year I was invited to several interdenominational meetings which were held for the purpose of learning how to live the Christian life. These meetings were organized and sponsored by ad hoc groups of lay people and were open to any interested Christians. Several hundreds of application letters were sent back from one three day meeting because of lack of space. (Seventeen hundred people from almost every state in the Union did attend.)

In starting new small groups, the 'older' Christians found themselves living their first year again and again with different people. Many of these group leaders have never had time themselves to penetrate the broad stream of our generation's corporate life and needs. They have never faced the *longer range* personal problems involved in the living out of one's life in changing family and age situations. The new groups had the danger of replacing involved evangelical *living* in the real world with a continuous evangelistic *programme*, which was a thing apart from the ordinary tasks and relations of secular life. It was an exciting but frothy life, and some of us yearned for the stability of the humdrum routine of living. We were caught up in a glorious treadmill of meetings and witnessing, which had become our lives.

On the other end of this religious spectrum there were the programme people of the institutional Church. Leaders in this group, who were often very suspicious of the new lay movement, were concentrating and redoubling their efforts almost entirely on religious education, corporate worship and responsibility, and social involvement. But these people seemed to be operating with the strangely blind assumption that laymen in the Church already have the kind of motivation to risk vulnerable involvement in the world—when they will not even support the Church's basic internal programme. And when

Hundreds of people were turned away from these meetings simply because the hotel accommodation was not available, and yet in almost no instances that I know about were there any promoting or advertising or any 'expense paid delegates'. Whatever one may say about the meeting content, there is little doubt that the participants were highly motivated. At least anyone who has tried to get a church weekend conference together would tend to think so.

their passionate pleading for involvement has met with stubborn silence, the resulting frustration in ministers' lives has been dreadful to behold. So as I looked around, I saw those of us in the lay awakening concentrating so hard on the necessary 'beginnings' that we were starting to look to the rest of the Church like a new and joyfully motivated nation of 'spiritual midgets'. And the institutional Church, in its horror at what appeared to be an anti-intellectual renegade spirit, was concentrating so hard on 'educating' people who had never been born, that they were producing a grim and cynical company of 'walking dead men'. They were finding little of the winsome and motivating joy of living and loving which has always marked the Christian Way. And the lines of tension between these two groups had been drawn.

Many institutional churchmen have been deeply disturbed by the apparently self-centred 'small groupism' and 'happy talk' of the newly converted Christians. The new Christians, on the other hand are appalled that the Church's programme has no way built into it to bring the people being ministered to into a personal reorientating relationship with the Living God and with each other —a relationship which is more than outward form. And neither side is attractive to the other. New Christians ask me, 'Why should I want to go back to the cold rejecting, cynical Church (which will not take me seriously as a person)?' On the other hand 'churchmen' say about the new group: 'Can't they see that their lives are being lived in an unreal cocoon—that they must burst out into the world to be fully Christ's people.' But the baffling part of this separation is that many members of *both* groups think that they have *already been on the other side and that the other side is a blind alley.* For instance, many of the education-social involvement people have rebelled against a childhood spent in the midst of inflexible legalistic men and women who had claimed that all you have to do is 'give your life to Jesus' and you are in—you are safe and free from the awful, sinful, world. On the other hand some of us who were raised in a liberal, pragmatic atmosphere tried to 'do good works', and life was really no different for the people we helped. We just frustrated them by giving them a clearer vision of what they did not have. Our good works just put elastoplast on cancers and either made us feel superior (at least we were *doing* something) or left us disillusioned, or both. And the people's lives were not changed so that they could creatively help themselves. But now it seemed to me that the truth was that *both* sides had correctly pointed out the dangers of the other's stance, while *missing* the essence of the other's reality—the lack of which is blocking both factions in their struggles for wholeness under God.

When I began to see the extent to which both groups were right in their criticisms of each other, I knew that the time had come for me to take a step. This was when I thought of turning back to the Church and coming home emotionally to its life. I had seen literally hundreds of men and women, many of whom had never been active in the Church, come alive and begin finding purpose, direction, and personal involvement in their own worlds. But who was going to bring them up? At conferences we could give them materials and suggestions on how to get started, but we knew that if each man was to discover his own place, the unique form of his own obedience in the world, he would have to find a group with lasting continuity in his own community.

This would have to be a continuing fellowship in which he could learn to walk through the tragedies, changes, and inevitable human encounters through the years. Such groups could provide centres of hope in different communities, as Paul's groups did in the early Church – small centres through which people, as seriously and personally committed Christians, could come to grips with the problems of their lives and the urgent issues of our time.

When I looked back at the Church, it was with a feeling of ambivalence. On one hand, I felt a vague repentance for the immature and defensive scorn I had felt. But on the other hand, I now had a calm realization that many of the ministers and laymen in the Church simply cannot imagine the nature and extent of the 'grass roots' reformation taking place all around us. They cannot see from the outside the power, hope, and integrity being generated in the lives of growing thousands of people. I saw that the Church cannot be the Church without a company of men and women with drastically changed purposes and directions, deeply motivated to be a servant people devoted to their Lord. But I also saw that the evangelical awakening cannot become a mature reformation until it leads people into the brokenness and alienation of the secular world. The only two alternatives I could see for me were: (1) to get *someone* to start another denomination, or (2) to get back into my own.

When I did start to go back, I learned a strange thing. For years I had been very suspicious of ministers because I had been deeply hurt by a few. I remember several years ago being asked to speak to an annual clergy conference in the diocese in which we lived. I came to the conference with some reservations. And as I looked around and chatted with the ministers, I remember thinking: *what a hostile bunch!* I had the feeling that they really thought the lay renewal bit was naïve. After I spoke that evening, there seemed to be a much cooler atmosphere. I decided that they were after me. I cannot help smiling as I write this. Recently I addressed the men of the same diocese and many of the same clergy were present. I had to tell them that it had taken three years, and a year and half of graduate study in psychology, for me to realize that it was *I* who was after *them*. And although I had not known it at the time, this was true. I had been so afraid of being rejected that I looked for—and consequently found—rejection coming from them. And of course some *was*. But what I did not see was that it was my suspicious and largely unconscious judgment of them which brought on a good bit of the lack of openness on their part. Since that meeting, several ministers have confessed the same experience from the other side of the issue—after realizing that their own unconscious rejection of new lay Christians, who have been 'turned on' outside their programme, has brought on much of the trouble they have had in their churches. It is amazing how many more ministers I meet these days who are interested in the Church renewal.

Now I was beginning to see how both we on the 'outside' in the lay renewal and those in institutional programme groups had been telling the Lord that the other group's members had taken the first bite of the apple in the garden. But now I was starting back into the orchard.

Chapter 11

COMING HOME TO THE ORCHARD . . .
THE APPLE TREE IS STILL THERE

*'. . . he will not let you be tempted beyond your
strength, but with the temptation will also provide
the way of escape . . .'*
                        I CORINTHIANS 10: 13 (RSV)

In coming back to a more emotionally involved role in
the institutional Church, I had to take a new look at the
old problems which had caused me to leave in the first
place. I had never left physically, having belonged,
attended and given regularly to the church all along,
but my real interest had left. The old problems I had
seen were still there: problems like, 'Why is there so
much confusion concerning what we are about in the
life of the Church?' And, 'Why is it so difficult for us
laymen to really go all out for the programmes we do
decide on in our church meetings?' It was not until
this past year that I began to see what these problems
have actually meant in my life.

I had been asked to speak to a group made up primarily of ministers in Boston. My job was to talk about
how a layman can really be a Christian in the Church,
beyond attending the worship services. I was excited
about going (Boston is a long way from South Texas),
and I wanted very much to do well. But I could not
prepare and kept putting it off. Finally, the day came

when I *had* to sit down and write my talk. But I could not write. I sat at my desk, paralysed, staring at the blank paper for almost an hour. I began to sweat. Perhaps nothing would come to me. But, while sitting there, I saw that I was facing my own question in a horribly real way. Here the church had given me an assignment in its programme—an assignment I wanted to do. Yet, I still could not get myself moving. As I sat there, I asked myself 'why?' What was on my mind that was keeping me from being engaged in the programme before me? I began to examine my thoughts during the previous hour—and I was ashamed. Do you know what I had been thinking? On the same programme of the session at which I was to address the conference there was to be another speaker. This man is a person whom I consider to be one of the most articulate and loving spokesmen for Christ in our time, particularly with regard to the problems of the laity. He was to *precede* me on the same platform without so much as a hymn between us, *speaking on the same subject which I was assigned.* I realized as I sat at my desk that what was going through my mind was the fear that *I might not look too good following Dr. Kenneth Chafin!*

Here I was, a consciously committed Christian, going fifteen hundred miles to tell a group of men about the liberating love of Christ, yet I could not prepare my address because my mind was occupied with how *I* was going to look. I tried to recall what else I had been thinking about during my hour of paralysis. I remember that I had been trying to figure out how I might capture these men's imaginations for Christ. This seemed much more noble than my previous thoughts until I had to ask myself, 'Or do you want to capture them for yourself?' And, of course, I never did know for sure. But as I sat there I began to see something else. I realized that perhaps *here* was the critical problem, the reason I had not been able to really throw myself into the church's programme; I had always had some much more fearful and threatening inner problems which had to be dealt with *before* I was free to even begin to be personally involved in the larger programme of the church with integrity. And those personal problems and doubts made me very uneasy about speaking for the living Christ without being a hypocrite.

What has apparently happened is that those of us who have been in policy-making positions in local churches have made some very faulty assumptions about laymen and the Church. We have assumed that a man's presence at committee meetings indicates a deep personal commitment to God and His purposes. We have assumed that these men have a freedom from self-centredness and fear of other people's opinions. We have *acted as if we* believed that they are ready to go out and openly share the freedom and understanding of their faith (which they are presumed to have), if only we could come up with the right vehicle for them, the right programme. *But it is not so!* At least for me and for dozens of men whom I have asked in moments of honest sharing, these assumptions simply *are not true.* Most of us had not been elected to church committees for qualities of dynamic personal and loving Christian involvement with people. Some were elected because of financial success. Others, the minister had asked to stand. Some were elected to keep the 'spiritual element' (or even the minister) from going off at half cock. Many of those elected saw the committee's function as a sort of financial advisory board to which the minister was to provide the spiritual direction (when there was time). For others membership was an honour, like other civic honours.

Most of us did not have any clear conscious picture of what it might mean for us to be *really* committed Christians in our world. And yet the ministers assumed that we were the spiritual centre of the church. But the truth was that most of us did not even know what the central human problems of alienation were—to which the Gospel might speak in the world. Because we did not know how to do that for which we were supposedly formed, we either became a rubber stamp group whose main purpose was to get the meeting time shortened, or we had long arguments primarily over financial issues, in which the lack of real communication was at least notable. We were often very frustrated, because we could not even pin down our own basic problems and disagreements.

But if all this is only partly true, and a person is deeply interested, how would he begin to find out what the real problems in the Church are?

About a year ago I was doing some studies in motivation and perception, and I began to realize that people do not necessarily respond to the facts before them, but rather they respond to what they *perceive* before them. And what I perceive *is* reality for me in determining my responses, even if my perception is *incorrect*. A classic example of what I am saying is the story of the two men travelling at night in the brushland of the Southwest of the United States. The driver lived on a ranch in the area, but the passenger was a stranger from the East.

Suddenly, as they approached a cut through a hill the Easterner saw in the headlights a boulder rolling down into the road ahead of them. He yelled, clambered toward the back seat and covered his face. The driver, on the other hand drove on without a sign of any disturbance because he knew that the 'boulder' was a tumbleweed. Both men had seen the same object, and both had reacted appropriately to what they saw. Yet one almost had a fit, whilst the other's blood pressure did not even change, because one man had been living where he could see and handle tumbleweed, and the other had not.[1]

I think this is what has happened in the whole business of Church renewal in many cases: Some ministers and church people have seen the restless stirring among laymen and the clamour for 'change' and 'honesty'. But because of their past experience with cliques of gossips and malcontents these ministers may *perceive* unsponsored lay activities as irresponsible and almost have a fit at the perceived danger.

I have been frustrated for years in trying to understand the basic problems we have in local church programmes because I have not known a simple fact about the way we, as people, solve problems—any kind of problems. For instance, imagine that you and I are assigned a simple problem in arithmetic to solve. Actually let us say that there are three of us. One of you is an ordained minister and the other a layman. I am standing before you with a blackboard behind me. On this blackboard I write with white chalk this simple problem:

1. This analogy has been adapted from that used by Donald Snygg and Arthur W. Combs in *Individual Behaviour: A New Frame of Reference for Psychology*. New York: Harper and Bros., Inc., 1949.

9
8
—

Then, let us say that I ask you to give me the first answer that pops into your head. When I actually did this, the minister came up with the answer '1'. I turned to the layman and asked him what answer he got. Without hesitation he said '72'. With the *same given information* the minister's and the layman's answer were 7100% apart. What had happened? Both men laughed as they realized that one had unconsciously *assumed* that it was a subtraction problem $(9-8=1)$ and the other had *assumed* that it was a multiplication problem $(9 \times 8 = 72)$, al-although I had given *no* sign to indicate that it was either. And each was correct from his own perspective. Before one can solve any problem, he evidently brings from his past experience an opinion or presupposition as to what the problem is, and this determines and limits his answer to the problem in a real way, even though the presupposition is usually unconscious or at least unexamined.

I believe that this is the cause of a good deal of the uncanny frustration and discord in our church meetings, and even between denominations. Each of us comes into such meetings with preconceived ideas about what it means to be a Christian, most of which are not even conscious. And these different ideas about what constitutes Christian living and purpose become the 'signs' which we unconsciously affix to every problem. And these often buried ideas become the stubborn personal criteria against which we unconsciously check the items which come up for consideration.

When this hit me, I realized why it has been so difficult to communicate about the life-changing experiences many people are having in the Church today. Although the stalwart churchman understands the *words* the new Christian uses to describe his new life, he sees in these words entirely different *meanings*. Without realizing it he has from his past put a negative 'sign' on words like 'conversion', 'witness', 'evangelism'. But the new Christian's 'sign' is very positive regarding these terms. So, looking at the same word symbols, the two get totally different 'answers' about the value of the experience described.[2] And this difference carries over into the conducting of church programme planning. Since we have not self-consciously examined these assumptions, for the most part, all we know consciously is that a proposed action 'doesn't sound right to me'. Yet we cannot give adequate reasons for our objections, so they sound like a personal rejection of the *person* submitting the plan. An argument ensues in which our logical reasons often sound weak, even to us, but our stubborn sense of being right is very strong.

What then is the solution? In coming back into the problems of being identified with the Church, I have found that the thing which has helped me most is that during these past few years I have begun to become *conscious* of what I think it actually does mean to live and grow as a Christian. I have begun to believe that the Christian life is a *pilgrimage*, not a *programme*; a pil-

2. As Piet Hein, the Danish poet and scientist put it in another context, 'Ideas go in and out of words as air goes in and out of a room with all windows and doors widely open.' *Life*, October 14, 1966.

grimage with people who want to be willing to love, live, and possibly die for Christ, each other, and the world. I have begun to experience what it is like to take the risk of revealing *my* true needs, and to love other Christians enough to let them *help me* when I am really hurt—as well as trying to help them. And built into this life is a yearning to share with others the freedom and healing one is finding. To know these things is giving a possible unity and direction to my whole life and to all the programmes of the church in which I am involved.[3] And when there are choices to be made about programme, these criteria help me to evaluate where I should invest my time.

I'm beginning to believe that before we can formulate programmes in the Church which will affect anyone's real life situation, we will have to be educated in such an atmosphere that our inherited *perceptions* about the whole Christian enterprise can change. I feel that we need to look at Christian Education in the Church with new eyes.

3. I have described this experience of becoming aware of what it meant to me to begin living the Christian life in *The Taste of New Wine*, Waco: Word Books, Inc., 1965, and Word Books, London, 1970.

Chapter 12

CHRISTIAN EDUCATION—
CAN THESE BONES LIVE?

'And I will . . . cover you with skin, and put breath in you, and you shall live . . .'

Ezekiel 37: 6 (RSV)

What if this is true—that we can begin living in a whole new perspective? What if this is not just the subjective pilgrimage of a few laymen, but instead is a valid approach to living the Christian life? How would this new perspective affect the whole matter of Christian education in the local church?

As I have spoken informally with persons in charge of Christian education for local parishes, on regional and national denominational levels, and with professors of Christian education in graduate theological seminaries, I have come away with some different insights into several of the basic problems. The men and women who write the programmes for the denominations are usually very competent people and they seem to be committed to the programmes they produce. When they test their material on pilot groups, they are often gratified with the results. But the breakdown seems to come in the local church after general distribution, leaving local educators frustrated and feeling inadequate (since they have been assured that all the materials have been tested in 'representative groups'), and leaving the programme

authors frustrated and stumped because their well-written, pilot-tested, programmes have flopped—*nationally.*
Not knowing what to do or say, everyone just pretends it isn't so and grinds ahead. In private, the lay teachers blame the material and the authors condemn the ineptitude and laziness of the local teachers and lack of support from the local ministers and Christian education people. The latter are caught in between, leaning one way or the other. But, as I was wrestling with this problem one day, I recalled an incident from my childhood which made me see the whole situation differently.

There was a little boy living in our neighbourhood when I was a youngster whom I shall call Henry. Henry didn't like me very much, and I thought he was a sort of hardheaded fat boy. But since there were not many other boys in the neighbourhood of our age we often had to play with each other out of desperation. I was active, interested in outdoor sports, and had a vivid imagination which I often used in playing 'guns'. I especially liked to play 'explorer along the Amazon in search of gold'. One day while wandering down by a creek after heavy rain, I found a children's old wooden slide which had been washed down in a flood. It was about seven feet long and when laid out flat on the ground made a perfect toy dugout canoe for paddling up the Amazon through the jungle. With great effort I dragged it home. Then I asked Henry to come over and play. Because of the cannibals along the Amazon, I needed someone to paddle the canoe while I shot natives to protect us until we could get to where the gold was. Henry was not very enthusiastic. He was more the practical type and liked to play games like 'shop'. I suspected even then that Henry could never really see the cannibals peeping out of those trees and bushes but he was so bored that he came over. We loaded our canoe with all kinds of imaginary supplies and pushed off on our journey. I was very excited. And sure enough, we had no more than rounded the bend from the embarkation camp when those little pigmy devils began to shoot at us with their poison darts from the trees! Very involved, I reached for my gun and began to pick them off from behind, telling Henry to 'paddle like mad!' But in a few moments in the thick of battle, with poison darts flying all around us, I heard my paddler talking in a very soft, kindly manner to someone whom I could not see. I stopped and listened; and Henry Jones was *selling groceries* to old ladies out of the front of my dugout canoe. He thought it was a country store in Oklahoma! I was furious! And after much argument, we finally just had to call it quits and not play together. We realized that we simply weren't on the same adventure.

As I chuckled, remembering my frustration at Henry's stubborn unco-operativeness, I began to see what may have happened in our denominational Christian education efforts. The lay people who are asked to teach and to learn the materials simply aren't on the same adventure in the same part of the jungle as the centrally located denominational leaders who are writing the materials. Most of the latter are ministers, many of whom have been chosen for outstanding work in local churches; but now that they have been called into the central office, they are on a *different personal adventure*. Their pride is at stake in a different way. Now they are called on to *produce materials*, rather than *lead expeditions*. They are not writing from the same canoe with the layman who is busy wanting to know how to dodge those poison darts and crocodiles. Their work is now being judged by academic standards and by a board, the members of which have emotional investments in certain theological positions. Of course, the messages from back in New York may be very relevant and helpful, but psychologically, the layman seems more likely to change his behaviour as a result of plans suggested by those he feels are also *likely to get killed trying them*. I think this personal vulnerability of the teacher is a key requirement for life-changing Christian education. And I think this has always been true.[1]

Look at some of the greatest Christian educators in the Church's history (Paul, Augustine, Luther, and Wesley . . . not to mention Jesus of Nazareth). These men wrote and taught from the front line. No one in their bands was more vulnerable than they. They were beaten, imprisoned, rejected, and some were martyred. And I believe it was partially because they were writing and speaking from the thick of the battle and their Lord was sustaining them, that men were willing to follow that Lord and His adventure—even at the risk of death. I think young men and women today are crying out for something to devote their lives to that is worth dying for. But they seem strangely unwilling to follow any leader who is not ready to be vulnerable to the world and to 'risk it' *with them*.

In thinking about my own role as a 'professional' Christian, I now realize something I had never thought of

1. Of course, I realize that many Christian educators have maintained their perspective and integrity. But I know from personal experience that peer group pressure, intellectual pride, and the self-protective tendency make it hard for me to have the same freedom in writing that one has 'on his feet' trying to help solve problems as they occur.

before. I have seen that the very fact that I find myself in a pulpit or on a platform witnessing to large numbers of people, gives me a source of strength in my Christian life which the man *listening* to me speak does not have. The mere fact that I am 'on the programme' means that people are giving me a special kind of emotional and psychological support, which helps me to continue to live and witness when I get discouraged. People, by listening, are taking me seriously as a human being and verifying my faith and insights unconsciously by their attention. And now, when I am tempted to tell people how they ought to witness in their businesses and communities, I remember that many of them are alone and do not have the public and the ego-encouraging platform of the religious setting in which to witness.

Incidently, this same thing may happen to 'pilot groups' trying out new Christian education programmes. That is, the simple fact that they have been chosen and are being watched gives them an incentive to learn plus an involvement with the programme and its authors which *later groups do not have.* This may account for the paradoxical 'success-failure' transition from pilot group to ordinary parish.

What I am thinking, I suppose, is that as I have travelled around, spoken, and led seminars and flown back every week to teach an adult class in my church, I have found that it is one thing to fly into the jungle, shoot a tiger, and fly out again, but quite another thing to move into the jungle and live with the tigers every day as the natives have to do.

Am I suggesting that Christian educators give up their vocations and that lecturers and evangelists stop travelling? Of course *not!* But I am suggesting that anyone who hopes to have the people he is teaching make a transition from *passive listening* to *active loving, must teach and witness primarily out of his own personal adventure of faith*. I am *not* suggesting subjective *content*. I am saying that as you are teaching any course, say a course in 'the prophets of the Old Testament' or 'social issues of the 1960's', that along with the content, you tell the people what the study and the involvement with the material *means to you* in your life now—how this study has excited your mind or changed your relationships. And if the subject has not helped *you* to more adequacy in your own pilgrimage as a person, or captured *your* imagination, then I would question whether this should be taught *by you* in the church Christian education programme. Let someone teach that to whom it has relevant existential meaning. There is a real place for academic learning for scholarship's sake, but I do *not think that place is in the Christian education programme of the average local congregation*. Time is *very limited* for the contact between teacher and lay students in the church's educational opportunities, and a very real choice must be made about this issue.

The churches—liberal and conservative—have tried, with different materials, to re-emphasize sounder, more sophisticated and varied educational programmes; but most of the people simply do not seem to find them relevant. And it does no good to blame the people. Besides, they have a deep intuitive grasp of the fact that Christianity is a *life* first, and only in a secondary sense, an academic encounter. You may say that the type of teaching I am pointing to will lead to an unbalanced programme dependent on the personal experience of the teacher. Who says so? What we are now calling a 'balanced programme' was at some time an arbitrary decision made by a man or group of men who were themselves incomplete. Our generation is not bound by someone else's ideas of balance (especially when they are no longer effective). But we *must know our history* if we are to live this way, as Santayana so wisely pointed out: 'Those who do not remember the past are condemned to relive it.' If God is real and the Holy Spirit is the real Teacher in the Church, then we cannot take ourselves too seriously as having to teach an entire college syllabus to all people. I do not believe the average layman's problem is a lack of information anyway. It is a lack of *motivation*. And if a man truly changes his direction and begins to try to live his *whole life* from Christ's perspective, he *will*, on his *own*, begin to seek to learn more about his faith—until he gains something of the breadth, wholeness, and balance God has for him. And, on his own, he will call for books and seminars and set them up—as laymen are doing all over the world today. But until he finds a continuing *motivation to search*, through a life which daily brings up new and threatening problems, I do not believe he will pay the price to seek, because the focus of his attention will be elsewhere.

But if motivation is one of the basic problems in Christian Education programmes, then how does an average lay teacher, or any Christian teacher begin to get his class members involved so that they can get caught up in the larger adventure of living creatively for Christ?

Chapter 13

ADVENTURE TEACHING . . .
THE PROBLEM OF INVOLVEMENT

'Immediately they left their nets and followed him.'
Matthew 4: 20 (RSV)

A few years ago I stopped and asked myself what kind of situations and group leaders get *me* involved. Since I am very self-centred, I have always been cautious about becoming involved in other people's programmes. As I looked at the effect of various teachers on my life, I began to see that when one is approaching a new *group* of people in a teaching situation, he is paradoxically approaching each person *individually* at first—though he may be speaking to the individuals as a group.

Think back and recall how you felt on the first day of a new class, or your first committee meeting. When I am a new member of such a group, I am always a little wary. Sometimes I have come to the meeting out of a sense of duty. But sometimes I am conscious of a kind of restless excitement inside, wondering if this situation will be something I can grasp and one which will interest me or change things in my life. If the announced subject is something in which I am predisposed to be interested, I want to be accepted as an adequate member of the group and be taken seriously as a person. And I will be a little nervous about my participation until I feel accepted. Until I am able to anticipate a place or task that I can feel is for me with my limitations in the larger movement and direction of the group, I will not be involved deeply nor will I take the risk of really being vulnerable with the group—much less for it. People who say we must do away with the approach to individuals in favour of a corporate approach are, it seems to me, almost unbelievably naïve about man's personal religious needs and response habits. As Sangster put it, 'to talk of the group mind is to talk in metaphor'.[1] Each man, if he decides to participate in anything, does so as an individual.

What I am saying is that, in my opinion, all of this talk to the effect that 'the people in the church should put the church's programme before their own petty individual spiritual needs', is extremely naïve and based on a false notion that man is unselfish and will tend to prove it if only given the chance. Historically, Christians have believed that we are all centred in ourselves and are sinful (See Genesis 3, Romans 3:23, etc.). I have found, to my horror at first, that I and the Christians with whom I have worked are basically selfish people. Most of us are motivated to work in the church and help others, not because we are good, but because we are experiencing, individually and personally, the loving acceptance of Christ and some of His people; and it is the greatest thing we have found in life. And this love and acceptance through Christ makes us *want* to be loving and unselfish toward others.

Consequently, a Christian teacher may fail to provide the conditions for sacrificial *corporate* action unless he can present his material and his vision in such a way

1. W. E. Sangster, *Let Me Commend*, London: Epworth Press, 1961.

that each person in the group can anticipate the security of a personal 'place'—some measure of acceptance of himself with his kinds of limitations. A person must, in a sense, see an emotional or spiritual 'way of living' on this team which his imagination tells him he can try out. That is, the proposed involvement must, in a real sense, be seen as a specific kind of involvement 'with his name on it'. This is *not* coddling and producing weakness. For once a person feels that he is accepted and that his life can somehow have more meaning because of the venture, then he will take his chances with the rest of us and almost enjoy the dangers. For then we are all shipmates, and each of us has taken the risk together to cast off from our other securities.

Paradoxically, it is *together* that we are *each* going to find his destiny. The Christian pilgrimage is a joint adventure; but to last, in my opinion, it must always remain an individual one for each of us. I think that the wreckage of many Christian education programmes can be attributed to the fact that a teacher or leader planned some programme that would be 'good for the group'. He brought it before the members for approval; and, not having any alternative programme the group casually voted its approval.

But then the poor leader was amazed and bitter when the members would not participate. They weren't against the programme. They just did not show up. I now feel that such a teacher may have failed to realize that the programme was a part of *his* personal adventure, and it never became that for the individual members of his group. It seems to me that this is why so many people have their fondest memories of church life centred around a time when a few were trying to build a congregation or even a church building. It was an adventure in which each one personally felt he had a part—and something died when the job was completed and the church could pay for the work to be done, the doing of which had given the early members a berth on the voyage, on the adventure. This may be one reason many of us in the Church have built building after church building—because we know of no other way to get people involved in a corporate adventure.

By being conscious of the need each person has to be a participating part of the movement of the group, the teacher is *not* calling for a sort of joint self-actualization project. The 'self-actualization' or 'self-fulfilment' which *does* occur on this type of pilgrimage is produced unconsciously when members of a Christian group get interested in the struggles and pain of living for Christ. Sooner or later they find themselves drawn beyond their own horizons toward the fulfilling of a potential meaning they see in lives and situations around them—beyond the walls of their own groups.

'Peace,' or a lack of tension, is not the goal of what I have termed *adventure teaching*, but rather it is finding together a participating perspective of loving wholeness in the world under God. As Viktor Frankl has said, what man actually needs for wholeness 'is not a tensionless state but rather the striving and struggling for some goal worthy of him. What he needs is not the discharge of tension at any cost, but the call of a potential meaning waiting to be fulfilled by him.'[2] And when a Christian pilgrim begins to grasp the idea that in his Father's house there are many places, including a place for him

2. Viktor E. Frankl, *Op. Cit.*, p. 166.

particularly in which he can have a unique part in God's creative action in history, then the teacher's task is sheer joy—and hard work. When I realized that there was a 'place' for me, a Christian way for me to live, I became tremendously keen to find out what form this adventurous living would take in my own life and experience. And as I began to try to live my life in God's perspective with others who were struggling to do the same, I found that Christ seemed to be calling us to an attitude of creative adventure. A realization of our acceptance of Him seemed to be followed by a tentative, vulnerable risking of self to accept others; and that leads to the possible discovery of a particular channel of emphasis in which our lives will flow into the future.

When we talk of the matter of 'Christian education in the local church', I think we are talking about *training for the adventure of living this life* by the bringing together of fellow adventurers. Each adventurer brings the needs and witness of his own pilgrimage. Each one already wants to find out all he can about God and about Christ and His character and purposes, not so that he can impress other people, but so that he can find out how to cope with the problems of living out this adventure on which he has embarked in the real world. He is, in fact, tremendously eager and thus teachable—*if* the content is presented in relation to the life.

If the material is to be examined in relationship to the adventure of Christian living, then it becomes all the more important that the teacher takes the time to orientate his students from the outset by telling the class something of his own Christian pilgrimage. I have come to believe that everyone is living some adventure, however dull or unadventurous it may seem to him. As a teacher, I must continually ask myself, 'On what adventures are my students living which would bring them to this class?' And I must look into my own *real* and *current* struggles and ask myself, 'What are the problems in our adventures which are related to the common frailty and humanity we all share?'

However, if the students are not on the *Christian* adventure, then it can first be presented to them as a way they must accept (at least hypothetically) in order to assimilate the meanings of the Christian teaching, which at its best has always been addressed to the problems of real life. To present material from an historical or systematically theological perspective to people without a basic philosophical background and who are not deeply involved in the Christian pilgrimage will leave most of them cold. Only those who are already historically and theologically inclined will be interested. I am more and more convinced that laymen are wrapped up in the problems and joys of *living* and *dying* as I think they *should* be in the same way as our Lord.

Strangely enough, I have found that often this taking of an hypothesis by the learner—that God was in Christ —for the purpose of investigating the Christian life has been the first conscious commitment of faith many adult Christians have made. And when they *do* assume that God is alive and that He wants to give them a creative and loving way to live and to find meaning in the chaos of modern life, then it is amazing the way they may, by this simple act of faith, become enthusiastic members of the venture on which your class is designed to take them. The experiences of the other Christians may then come alive to them. They can begin to give up their negative assumptions and see the faith from the *inside*, the point from which eventually it *must* be seen. The emphasis then changes for me as teacher from a displaying of my knowledge about the subject to a *relating* of that knowledge to the problems of living for God. This relating can either focus on the life situation out of which an historical event arose, or on the *living problems* which brought up a theological controversy of the past.

One who uses this approach must change his teaching style to re-stating all he knows in terms of the life of Christians. And it can be done, although it takes a lot of work and a great deal of self-examination. It means, in fact, that a teacher must be on the same adventure as the students and that he must face with them the fact that he may be far behind many of them, not only in his knowledge, but in his ability to *live* that knowledge in the context of the current problems of *his own* life. To admit this inadequacy honestly is very dangerous for a teacher, or anyone else. But it provides a 'floor of vulnerability' down to which it becomes safe for a class member to be honest. And except in rare instances a group will never be more open and vulnerable than its leader. In this way a teacher can release the 'power of the personal' into the life of the group.

I have found that almost everyone is interested in life and how to live it. Jesus dealt almost exclusively with the nature of God's kingdom or reign in terms of how it would be illustrated in real life situations. The subject matter is very earthy and secular, often dealing with areas of life we would consider crude or even nasty in church meetings.

Somehow we have soaked the Scriptures in such a

sugary religious solution that we only look at their symbolic meanings. We can no longer see the raw earthy *content* of the stories Jesus used to describe the nature and rule of God in His coming kingdom. We read these parables to our children for bedtime stories—but what are they dealing with in terms of human life? For instance, what is the content of the classic parable Christ used to describe the forgiving nature of God the Father for self-centred man? The story is about *a drunken whoremonger who ran away with his share of his father's money!* (See prodigal son: Luke 15: 12–23). Or when Jesus told us that our worship of God is not to be centred in the temple but that we are to worship Him in spirit and in truth—He was talking to a woman who had slept with so many different men she did not know which one to call her husband (See woman at the well: John 4: 1–30). In another place Jesus illustrated the vulnerable offering of God and the rejecting nature of His people in terms of a bunch of crooked businessmen who tried to steal a wine business by deceit, brutality, and murder (Story of the vineyard: Matthew 21: 33–41). These are honest earthy stories of real life through which Christ revealed the essence of His message.

I am NOT suggesting the starting of some sort of 'honesty cult'. Such groups are often harmful and almost invariably wind up being *un*Christian. The object of honesty in adventure teaching is not to reveal immoral and lascivious incidents. The object is rather to begin to acknowledge to God and to each other the true nature of the personal struggles of living in the world today, so that we can begin to find freedom, healing, and forgiveness—and provide a place where others can experience these things. One does not rip off his or anyone else's mask.

Rather he becomes willing for God to remove the unnecessary part of his façade gradually by providing the security he needs to be more honest. Also a ground rule in this type of group is never to share something in such a way that it may make *another* person vulnerable. The highest value in the Christian life is not honesty—but *love* (1 Corinthians 13). This is a very important basic difference between Christian joint-adventuring and some (humanistic) psychologically orientated groups.

I am suggesting that adventure teaching can get people involved in dealing with living situations like those used by Christ in revealing the nature of the Father and His kingdom. Further, the contemporary experiences of the genuinely committed members of an adventuring class, as they try each week to live for God experimentally, have a way of triggering unconsciously the 'hypothetical' Christian to get involved in his own life outside the group. And although this one will often not realize that his own life is changing, the others will. And when people see those with whom they are in personal contact being healed by God and transformed into more loving and committed persons, then there is a great quickening of faith which runs through the lives of everyone, including the leader. In Christ's meetings in the New Testament there seemed to have been a core of people who had been or were being healed. I am convinced that Christian education enterprises need this core of people who have been touched by Christ and who are sort of 'apprentice-seamen' risking failure to learn the ropes of living, as they continue the voyage itself.

Psychologically, in terms of motivation, I have found during these past ten years as a teacher and small group leader that 'going on an adventure' is a very different enterprise from 'learning an academic subject'. What is taught may at times be very scholarly, but to be relevant to the average layman it must speak to intellectual or emotional needs *sensed* by the class member. One of my greatest difficulties as a Christian teacher has been to give up certain theological terms in *adventure teaching*.

I was taught at college that we must educate the people to use these specialized words. But *who said we must?* If we have simpler words to express the same truth to un-trained laymen, *why not use them!* Otherwise we are training another secret society with another language which blocks the pilgrims in their communications with the world. In a sense, many theological colleges have already done this in blocking the future ministers in their communications with us. Many pastors who want to be involved in the new renewal in the Church are having a terribly hard time expressing themselves in ordinary language among groups of new Christians. Be-cause, for these new people the language of Christianity is simply the language of *living in relationship in the world*. If this insistence on teaching *all* Christians the philosophical jargon of systematic theology actually helped people to become more concerned with loving the world for God, I'd say do it at all costs—*but where is the evidence that it does?*

I think laymen desperately need *operational* models, examples of vulnerable concern in the flesh, to moti-vate them to begin to learn to *live* the truth of the Chris-tian perspective. I know that this approach will seem like a gross oversimplification to a professional educator's orderly mind. And it *is* oversimplified. But great teachers, like Dr. Karl Menninger encourage me to risk trying it by their example: 'It will be objected that this sharpness or clarity involves certain distortions or mis-interpretations, dependent upon oversimplification. But this is the perennial dilemma of the teacher: the teaching of facts and figures versus the teaching of truth. To convey a model, a teacher must reify the diagram and declare clearly what cannot be seen at all. The student must "learn" things in order to realize subsequently that they are *not* quite the way he learned them. But by that time he will have gotten into the spirit of the matter, and from this he may arrive at some approximation of the truth, an approximation he will continue to revise all his life long.'[3]

This is not a sermon on how Christian education should be accomplished. I am merely witnessing to one approach which has changed my own life and ministry profoundly. I believe that Christian education has to do with getting to know and worship the living God and participating in His action in the world. So I have been thrilled to see that as people have really started to get caught up in the vision and pilgrimage of living with Christ, then sooner or later, they have seen that, from Christ's perspective, the group members must move toward a deeper intellectual grasp of the truth and toward a purpose beyond the spiritual nurture of each member. As these individual Christians begin to see all of life from Christ's perspective, they start to discover real needs out in the world with their names on them. And it is through this natural process that what the church calls 'programme' may be born.

3. Karl Menninger, *Theory of Psychoanalytic Technique*, New York: Harper and Row, 1964, p. 14.

Chapter 14

FROM PIETY TO PROGRAMME . . .
IN THE CHURCH

'. . . How great a forest is set ablaze by a small fire'
James 3: 5 (RSV)

How does renewal and commitment get from a single changed person into a specific programme in the larger main stream of the Church's life? I have known some very winsome and powerful Christians, both ministers and laymen, whose lives have taken on a new radiance during the past few years. Some of these men and women are people with great natural abilities who had already succeeded in building churches, congregations and great organizational structures. But now these same leaders wanted their people to find *Life*. Watching their enthusiastic attempts to take the new style of life they have found and structure it into programmes, I have seen failure after failure—leading to frustration, division and gross misunderstanding on all sides.

Of course it goes without saying that any significant change in a parish programme will be deeply and sincerely opposed by some church members. This is a frightening world we are living in for a good many people. Think about it. Some members came stumbling into the church years ago out of some personal terror or private pit of guilt, or a hell on earth about which they have never told and hearing that God would forgive them or even that a loving God 'backed this club', they joined and found some sort of peace and security in a frightening world. They may never have heard about a personal faith in terms that seemed relevant to them, but the public worship—just as it is, or the quiet meetings, may have become the only recurring, dependable events in a life of chaos inside for them. And when some bright eyed young business people, or ministers, start talking with enthusiastic seriousness about a 'more committed' way to live, the old parishioners may perceive this 'new life' as a demand to give up something or confess openly some sin they have held back from God for years and do not want to change. Or this new approach might signify to the average parishioner a grim disciplined life with which he cannot begin to identify himself. He may sense that the new approach is going to do away with the stability of the psychological adjustment he has made with his terror or guilt. And if this new programme gets *in* and he can't go along, then he may be on the 'outside' again. Anyone who has ever really been afraid and alone and then found security, however tenuous, will understand why these people put up no small objection to a new approach which they don't understand or with which they cannot identify themselves. Other church members remember a certain religious excitement surrounding their own joining of the church, but since it 'wore off' for them, they assume it will for this new bunch. Of course some people are simply reactionary and do not like change. Still others have taken a cool look and do not agree that a change is necessary but I believe that the problem is deeper than any of these kinds of objections. I believe that we have made a significant historical mistake in our approach to renewal in the Church.

Church leaders have looked back at the great revivals of the past—at the way hundreds of thousands of people were deeply touched and their lives and behaviour significantly changed. These leaders have examined the methods which seemed to have brought about the astounding results at the high tide of renewal, and have carefully adapted these methods to the modern church's programme: direct study of the Bible from the Protestant Reformers; small commitment groups from the Wesleyan Revival; evangelistic preaching missions from the 18th and 19th century revivals in England and the United States—always updating, adapting, and putting them in modern terms. A denomination will get very excited about its 'new' programme and spend a fortune advertising and disseminating information so that everyone will understand. Six months later the leaders wonder how such a great idea could fail so miserably at the grass root level.

Several years ago I spent some time going back through the Church's history to try to see what did happen in the revival movements which seemed to have lasting integrity. But instead of looking at the methods and activities of each movement when it was *at its crest*, I tried to peel back the layers and see how these renewals *began* in each case. Because, for most of us, the problem is not how to sustain a renewal in the church, but how to *begin one*. As the evidence began to stack up, I came to a revealing conclusion. In most of the great vital movements in the Church's life a simple almost identical pattern unfolded. One person in a local situation—who was usually not very important at the time—decided to give himself wholly to God with no strings attached. Then a few others gathered around this person, because total conscious commitment by a sensitive individual evidently makes people somehow 'hungry' or 'homesick', for God. And as these few lives became deeply committed to the living Christ, a common vision came through the small group's life together which gave them the particular shape their obedience would take in the world. Up to this point in each group's development the institution usually had no idea who these people were. I began to realize that the beginnings of genuine renewal were *invisible to the Church at large*. But once the group members had committed themselves to the Lord and to each other and had experienced the common adventure of beginning to try to live wholly for Christ, *then* what the Church calls renewal began in all sorts of different ways, *depending on the needs the group saw in the world of its time* from its new perspective. Great numbers of people were then drawn to commit themselves to God and the purposes of the group. And great teaching, preaching, and movements to change social abuses poured new life into the Church.

Look at some of these people whose simple individual commitments were, through small adventure-type groups, the germinating seeds for corporate renewal: Paul, Patrick of Ireland, Augustine, Francis of Assisi, Luther, Ignatius Loyola, Wesley, George Fox, and many more. And how did renewal develop in the beginning through these men? Take any one of them. One of the least familiar for most Protestants is Ignatius Loyola (1491–1556). He was a professional soldier in Spain who, when he was in his twenties, was injured in battle. In the hospital he came across some devotional literature and became deeply converted. He committed his life to God and spent several years integrating the life of Christ into his militarily disciplined mind. He learned how to live his whole life in terms of his new faith. He was so controversial, yet outstanding, that he was sent to the University of Paris for further education. There 'in the dormitory', so to speak, by the depth and clarity of his commitment, he drew to himself a small group, half a dozen young men (one was a priest, as I recall). One of these young men was a baron's son named Francis Xavier, who was to become one of the greatest missionaries in the entire life of the Church. But as these men met, alone and virtually unknown to the institutional Church, they caught a vision of what it would mean for their own little group to live for Christ. And the Society of Jesus (Jesuits) was born. Whatever one may think about some of this group's political actions with regard to those of certain popes, it remains that they developed into one of the most powerful and widespread Christian teaching and foreign mission ministries in history.

Check the lives and renewals attributed to some of the other great Christian leaders and examine their beginnings. As I did this, it was interesting to note that none of those who later were known as renewers of the Church at the personal level (whom I encountered) *set out* to instigate a programme for *other people*, the way we so often do in trying to renew the Church. All of them were trying to find out how *they* could live sanely under God

and find out what they were supposed to do and to be.[1]
But historically, where these few deeply given lives have
not been present, 'renewal' has either been a political
manoeuvre, or it has been without an ethical and spiritual cutting edge to change the people's real behaviour
and social structures. I suppose the most clear example
of such a 'renewal' might be that of Henry VIII in England at the time of the Protestant Reformation in
Europe. But there *was* an inner-church renewal among
the people in the Church of England. Some two hundred
and twenty years later when John Wesley's 'heart was
strangely warmed', a Christian revival took place which
may well have saved England from a fate like that resulting from the French Revolution.

What this study of the vital awakenings of the past has
led me to see is that Christian renewal in the Church
does not look like that which I had been led to expect.
I had thought that the first and immediate sign of renewal in a local congregation would be an increase in
numbers. But I do not believe this is true. One of the
most significant contemporary experiences of personal
commitment to Christ in the Church and its involvement
in the world started twenty-one years ago with a congregation of nine people and no publicity. And now, although there were still less than 100 members when I was
there a few years ago, people come to the Church of the
Saviour in Washington, D. C., from all over the world

1. Although I am not including Karl Barth among the reformers listed above, I have always been interested in his comment with regard to the theological revolution his study in
Romans brought about. He is quoted as having said that he felt
like a man in a dark bell tower, groping to find his own way, who
had reached out to steady himself and was surprised to hear a
bell ringing.

to find out how to live in community.[2] I travelled almost a four thousand miles round trip for a weekend there and considered it a very valuable experience.

I am convinced that many renewal attempts have been ruined by being wooed to a premature numerical success. This is what I mean: If we are thinking that renewal will spring from a relationship with God which touches and potentially transforms *all* of one's ordinary human relationships, then the leaders of a renewal with this emphasis had better try this life themselves *together,* personally and privately, so that they will know the pain and joy of actually living every part of it. We had better learn how to be open with each other and God and have experienced the struggles this involves *firsthand.* Because if we haven't lived it awhile before large numbers of people come flooding in, we may find that our roles as leaders can make it very difficult to have enough real emotional privacy so that we can learn to *live* the life at all—rather than *publicly performing it*—the life we are telling other laymen to risk all in which to participate. I know some sad ministers with considerable ability who have 'gone for the renewal bit' and have made lots of people excited, only to find that they, themselves, really did not know how to lead their people to be open in small groups, for instance. They did not know, because they had never invested the time and energy to live in a small group as a *vulnerable, uncertain member.* I am becoming convinced that not just the great renewal movements of the past, but *any lasting* renewal, local or individual, takes place in this way. And I believe this learning first to live the life together without a pro-

2. See a description of this venture in *Call To Commitment* by Elizabeth O'Conner, New York: Harper and Row, 1963.

gramme is essential for another reason—because of the way authentic ventures for Christ seem to develop from this perspective.

When I have been in a prayer or study group in the church, we have often begun to feel guilty about just 'meeting for ourselves'. And we have decided that we must move out into the world to help in Christ's healing, reconciling ministry. So we have sometimes written on the blackboard several possible areas for service, usually listing projects in which we know other church groups are involved (e.g. coffee bars, racial integration programmes, etc.). Then after lengthy discussion, we have voted on what God's will would be for us and invariably I have been disappointed that nothing much happens.

But now I am beginning to see that if a group of people begin to live for God and try to see *all* of life from His vantage point, as this is revealed in Christ, their new perception causes a kind of sensitizing of their *vision*. I remember that certain bruised and broken situations, which I had seen around me for years and hardly noticed, began to disturb me deeply when I saw them from my new perspective. I found myself drawn to find out about such problems. And that which now made my heart ache to see, actually drew me toward involvement to help heal the brokenness or hurt I saw. As I have said in these last chapters, several years ago I looked around in the Church and saw the lonely apathetic people and committees. This lack of purpose began to disturb me. I realized that there *must* be a way for us to find and communicate life to each other in Christ's body. And the past ten years of my life have been given to the task of finding out all I could about these things. The

'programmes' which developed out of this personal striving to meet a specific need have included dozens of experimental small groups, the developing of weekend
conference programmes at a retreat centre called Laity
Lodge, and a good bit of speaking and writing to provide
materials for other people interested in the problem
which has captured my vocational attention and is filling
my life.

I guess I am trying to say that Christian programmes
and lives are not created by one's affinities or even by our
outward abilities. I believe that God calls us to *problems,*
not programmes, in which we will find our ministries—problems which captivate our minds and imaginations and motivate us to give our lives to try to bring
Christ's vision of wholeness to these situations and
people, as we begin to see them from His perspective.

Now I am a layman again, living in a suburban neighbourhood, teaching an adult class in a local church, and
meeting with a group of fellow strugglers on Monday
mornings trying to learn how to be God's person. As a
matter of fact, everything might seem to be very similar
to our situation years ago when we set out to find God's
will for our lives and yet nothing is the same. The people
and ministers of St. David's Church make up our spiritual home where we are experiencing God's love and renewal in the Church, which started quietly here years
before we came. It is from this home that I sometimes go
out to other church groups to *talk about* renewal instead
of having to get renewed away to be able to come home
and talk about it.

In the Monday morning strugglers' group, made up of
ministers and laymen and started by an attorney, two
building contractors, and a dentist, some of our lives

are being reshaped in ways we do not understand. We do know that this life together is making us want to live more fully for Christ's sake in the larger world around us—a world that is beginning to come into the focus of our present attention. The things which are happening in our lives would make another book, but I am finding with these men the hope and courage I have always needed to dare to try to see this day through Christ's eyes.

The question which really haunted me when I first read the parable about the blind man and Christ's second touch was: 'Can God really do it? Can Christ give the Christian Church a second touch, so that we can begin to see the world of the Personal. Can He really change life in this way in the materialistic twentieth century?' And during these past few months I have come to believe that He can ... and *is*, doing just that!

Several years ago a man, who has since become a dear friend, came to the end of his rope. He was in his thirties, he had been an active churchman for years, was very successful in his business life, had a wife and four children, and was contemplating suicide. This man, whom I shall call Jack, was driven to succeed at everything he did, but he hated the person he had become. At this point he met some people with whom he could identify deeply, except they acted as if their lives were just beginning, instead of ending. As a result of being with these people, Jack's life received a second touch. He decided that he would try to give his future to God, a day at a time. His wife made the same decision, and they prayed together about their lives. Jack just couldn't believe that God could really change a life as fouled up as he felt his was. And he said so. But he began by faith to learn to live with Christ as the Lord of his life. First, Jack tried to reach out to his family. When he started communicating as a person with his wife, she told him that he had been such a bear with the little ones that for years she had pushed them out of the front of the house when he came home from work. So Jack began to get to know his children.

About two weeks later his twelve-year-old son came in to talk to him. This boy had no friends at school and had begun to steal things from around the neighbourhood to get attention. He was almost totally alone. 'Dad,' he said hesitantly, 'what's happened to you lately?' His dad who had been a tough professional athlete looked up from his desk. 'Well, son,' he struggled for the right words, 'I—guess I was making a pretty big mess of my life and I decided I'd ask God to take it over and show me how to live it.'

The boy looked at him and then down at the floor. 'Dad,' he said quietly, 'I think I'd like to do that too.'

The father just stood there with tears running down his cheeks and he and the boy held each other and wept together. The next day Jack had to go to New York on a business trip for two weeks. On the way back he was anxious to get home. When his plane got in, his son broke through the crowd and ran out on the ramp to meet his father. His eyes were shining with excitement! Hugging him, he said breathlessly, in a kind of grateful wonder, 'Daddy, do you know what God has done?'

'No, what son?' his dad asked.

'He's changed every boy in my class!!'

Jack could not wait to tell me this story. 'I guess God *can* change the world,' he said smiling.

And I believe He can.